The Australian ETF Guide

HOW TO INVEST MORE CHEAPLY SIMPLY AND EFFECTIVELY USING EXCHANGE TRADED FUNDS (ETFs)

DAVID BASSANESE

The Australian ETF Guide:

*How to invest more cheaply simply
and effectively using exchange traded funds (ETFs)*

2016 Copyright: David Bassanese

I would like to acknowledge the help and support of my colleagues at BetaShares Capital for making this book possible, and especially that of Ilan Israelstam and Anton Allen for diligently reviewing early drafts.

That said, any remaining errors or omissions are my responsibility. I also note that this book was written in my personal capacity, and the opinions expressed here are my own and do not necessarily reflect those of BetaShares Capital Ltd.

ABOUT THE AUTHOR

David Bassanese is the Chief Economist of BetaShares, one of Australia's leading managers of exchange traded funds. David is a former senior financial columnist for *The Australian Financial Review* newspaper, and an interest rate strategist with Macquarie Bank. His is also a former Federal Treasury and OECD economist, and a graduate of Harvard University.

The first edition of this book was released in 2014 while David was working at *The Australian Financial Review*. In view of the rapid changes in the ETF industry in recent years, it was considered worthwhile producing this timely 2016 update.

WHAT READERS SAID ABOUT THE FIRST EDITION

"David's book let me know I was on the right track. I now see ETFs not as a blunt instrument, but rather a finely tuned product. David explains comprehensively their multitude of uses and opportunities they offer. There are gems of knowledge on virtually every page! David also explores and explains the stock market far more comprehensively than just explaining ETFs and his explanations will be useful for a long time to come."

Christopher, Sydney NSW

"This book is a must read for investors looking at diversifying into ETFs. For those already investing, it has a coverage and depth which will add to current knowledge and will provide a check against their strategies. For those who don't know David Bassanese's research the book will be a revelation. For those who do, it is a confirmation of his professionalism. I thoroughly recommend it to all interested in ETF investments."

James, Brisbane QLD

"As an investor in shares and property, I found I was sadly lacking in knowledge about ETF's – snippets in the papers and blogs not really providing enough depth. David's book has well and truly 'lifted the fog' – it is well written, concise, detailed enough without being too technical, and a great source of knowledge on the subject. I can move forward now on using ETFs more confidently in my investment decisions. Highly recommended"

Paul, Melbourne VIC

"I found the ETF book extremely informative and I have already made some initial investments."

Gordon, Adelaide SA

Advice Warning

DISCLAIMER

PROPRIETARY SERVICE

TABLE OF CONTENTS

Introduction: Why ETFs are an investor's best friend........... xxi

STEP 1 Appreciating the importance of good investments...1

We're getting older and living longer. 2

Achieving reliable investment returns remains difficult........... 3

Pensions and super concessions could be cut 5

Running an SMSF can be costly and complex............................ 7

Many investors still don't use ETFs.. 15

STEP 2: Understanding what ETFs are and how to use them..19

What am I investing in? The three key features of an ETF 20

ETF's Unique Structure 21

Other ETF Benefits.. 25

Cost 26

Diversification 29

Liquidity... 30

Fair Value 30

Asset Backing Security 31

Tax Advantages 31

Transparency...34

Survivorship Bias...34

ETF Concerns/Trading Tips 35

ETFs, ETPs, ETCs, and Exchange Traded Managed Fund.........35

ETFs 36

Structured Products...38

Managed Funds..39

Tracking Error 40

Spot vs. Futures Prices 42

Issuer Risk..44

Counterparty Risk 45

Liquidity and Bid-Offer Spreads 48

Where can you find the Intra-Day NAV?.....................50

Top tips on buying ETFs 51

Currency Exposure...52

International Taxation...54

Market Pricing and International Time Zones 56

STEP 3: Knowing what ETFs are available in

Australia 59

Global backdrop 60

Australian Market Overview.................................61

Australian Equity ETFs..66

Large Cap Weighted Australian Equity 66

Small Cap Australian Equity 70

Equal or Fundamentally-Weighted Australian Equity ETFs.....73

Australian Sector ETFs..77

Ethical ETFs.. 80

Bear (or Short) Funds... 81

Geared Funds.. 84

Managed Risk ETPs 89

High Yield ETPs 90

    BetaShares' Covered Call Strategy..................... 93

    BetaShares Dividend Harvester Fund 95

    Aurora Dividend Income Trust.......................... 98

Other "Strategic" or actively managed funds 99

International Equity ETPs 100

A Word on Currency Hedging.................................. 101

Global vs. Australian Performance........................... 102

Broad (Developed Country) International ETPs..................... 103

    Alternative weights 106

    Income Focused 107

    Actively Managed 107

    Managed Risk 108

World Ex-USA 109

United States 109

    S&P 500 Index 110

    Income Focused 112

    Other US Equity Indices 113

    Bear and Gear Funds... 114

Asian Equity ETFs.. 114

Europe.. 116

Emerging Markets.. 117

Global Sector ETFs 120

Australian Fixed Income ETFs... 122

Bond Market Basics.. 122

Bloomberg Composite Australian Bond Index 125

Bond Market ETFs.. 127

Corporate Bond Risk and Return 130

Indexed Bond ETFs 133

International Bond ETFs..136

Cash ETFs 139

Commodity ETPs 140

Broad Commodity ETPs 141

Gold ETFs 142

Other Commodity ETPs 144

Synthetic ETFs vs Structured Products 145

Hedged vs. Non-Hedged Commodity ETFs........................... 147

Futures vs Spot Prices 148

Foreign Currency ETFs 150

STEP 4: Developing ETF Investment Strategies.................. 153

Diversification within a Single Asset Class 154

Multi-Asset Class Portfolio...158

Strategic Asset Allocation.. 162

Tactical Asset Allocation 163

Fundamental or Valuation based strategies........................ 164

Momentum & Trend based strategies.................................. 168

A simple momentum and trend-based rotation strategy .. 170

Some caution on momentum models.................................... 172

Core/Satellite Investment Portfolios.................................175

Passive vs. Active Managed Funds 176

Equity Market Tilts 178

Trade Market Views with a Market ETF 178

Thematic Equity Tilts 181

Financials vs. Resources 181

High Dividend Stocks 183

Small vs. Large Caps 184

Domestic vs. International Equities 185

Emerging markets 187

China 188

Global Sectors 189

NASDAQ-100 Index 190

Bond Market Tilts **191**

Corporate vs. Government Bonds 191

Nominal vs. Inflation Protected Bonds 193

Local vs. International 195

Ad-Hoc Strategies **196**

Cash Equitisation 196

Tax Loss Harvesting 196

Conclusion **199**

INTRODUCTION: WHY ETFS ARE AN INVESTOR'S BEST FRIEND

With the wreckage of the burst American dotcom bubble and the sub-prime mortgage crisis just behind us, you could be forgiven for thinking that most financial market products these days are designed simply to fleece unsuspecting investors.

But, over the past decade, one product has emerged from fairly humble beginnings to shake up the established finance world. Initially intended only as a product for large institutional fund managers, it has been strongly embraced by retail investors.

The leading US investment magazine, *Barron's*, went so far as to argue that these products "probably rank as the most successful financial product of the past two decades."

And in an ironic twist, those who were the intended beneficiaries from this product's introduction – professional fund managers – are now having their cosy world threatened by the product's growing popularity among retail investors.

What is the product? We are talking about *exchange traded funds*, or "ETFs" for short.

At its heart, an ETF is nothing more than an index fund that trades on the stock market, and can be bought and sold just like an ordinary share. An ETF that tracks America's S&P 500 index, for example, is designed to rise or fall each day in line with the US S&P 500 market index, before fees and expenses. It should also pay dividends in line with that of the index each and every year.

ETFs can track the performance of selected equity, bond, or commodity indices, such as the S&P/ASX 200 Australian equity index, America's S&P 500 equity index, China's stock market, the MSCI Emerging Markets Equity Index, or even the gold price.

Simple right? As we'll see, ETFs have other attractive features for investors, especially compared with traditional managed funds that often don't try too hard to beat their benchmark index and can be very expensive. Indeed, especially for self-managed super funds (SMSFs), these relatively cheap and easy to understand investment products may be especially important. I'd go so far as to suggest that ETFs can be the SMSF investor's best friend!

As we'll see, ETFs allow investors to develop their own highly diversified core investment portfolio for a fraction of the price charged by active fund managers. There are also a wide variety of ETFs that enable investors to tactically tilt their portfolio toward certain asset classes or investment themes should they so desire.

However, ETFs are not without pitfalls. At face value, ETFs look simple, but their underlying structure – and as we'll see that of other ETF-like products - can be complicated, and present their own unique set of risks and challenges that investors need to be aware of. There are certain key issues that worry investors when it comes to ETFs. This book will explore these concerns, some of which are more valid than others. Rest assured: we'll equip you with the key strategies you'll need to use ETFs easily and safely in your portfolio.

This remainder of this book is divided into 4 easy steps.

Step 1 aims to highlight the importance of better investment options in the face of the growing challenges of saving adequately for retirement. We're all growing older and living longer, while at the same time, returns on traditional "safe" retirement investments have dwindled. That means the cost and effectiveness of our investment options matter even more – we can't take the future for granted.

Step 2 "looks under the hood" of ETFs in particular. It will help you familiarise yourself with what ETFs are exactly and how they can be properly bought and sold on the Australian Securities Exchange (ASX), just like an ordinary company share. This step will also introduce you to the myriad benefits ETFs offer investors and will hopefully allay some common misperceptions about their risks.

Step 3 then introduces the vast and growing range of ETFs currently available in Australia. Products are now offered which cover every major asset class, such as equities, bonds, commodities, and currencies – but also include a range of specific investment strategies.

Finally, **Step 4** outlines a range of ETF trading and investment strategies, such as how to use ETFs to build a cheap and highly diversified strategic asset allocation portfolio, and/or tactically invest in favoured industry sectors, geographic areas, or other investment themes.

Let's start at the beginning with **Step 1**. Welcome to the wonderful world of ETFs!

STEP 1

Appreciating the importance of good investments

WE'RE GETTING OLDER AND LIVING LONGER

At the crux of Australia's looming retirement investment challenge is the fact that, as in most of the developed world, our population is getting older, and we're living longer. According to the Australian Bureau of Statistics' latest estimates, the share of the population aged 55-years or older has almost doubled in the past 40 years, from 17% in June 1971 to 26.5% in June 2015[1].

Elderly Population Share

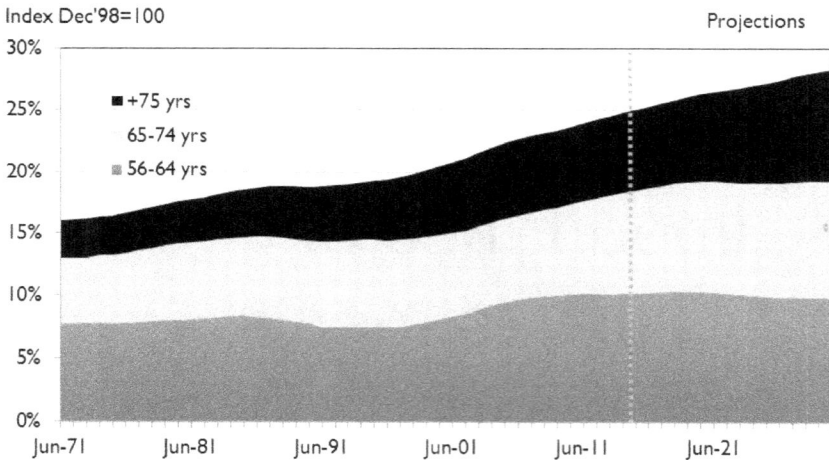

Source: ABS

What's more, the ABS projects this share will rise to approximately 30% over the next 20 years[2].

In terms of sheer numbers, there are already 6.3 million Australians aged 55 years or more, who are therefore either in or starting to

---

[1] Australian Bureau of Statistics, *Demographic Statistics*, June 2015. Cat. No.3101.0.

[2] Australian Bureau of Statistics, *Population Projections 2012-2101*, Cat. No. 3222.0

ponder retirement. This number is projected to grow to 8.6 million by June 2030. As of today, there are already 3.6 million Australians aged 65 years or older, with this number projected to grow to 5.6 million by June 2030.

We're also living longer. The average life expectancy for newborn children has increased by approximately 10 years over the past 40 years – to 80 years for males, and 84 years for females. As of today, the approximate average life expectancy for those aged 55 years is another 30 years, and for those aged 65 years, it is another 20 years.

Expected Remaining Years of Life by Current Age

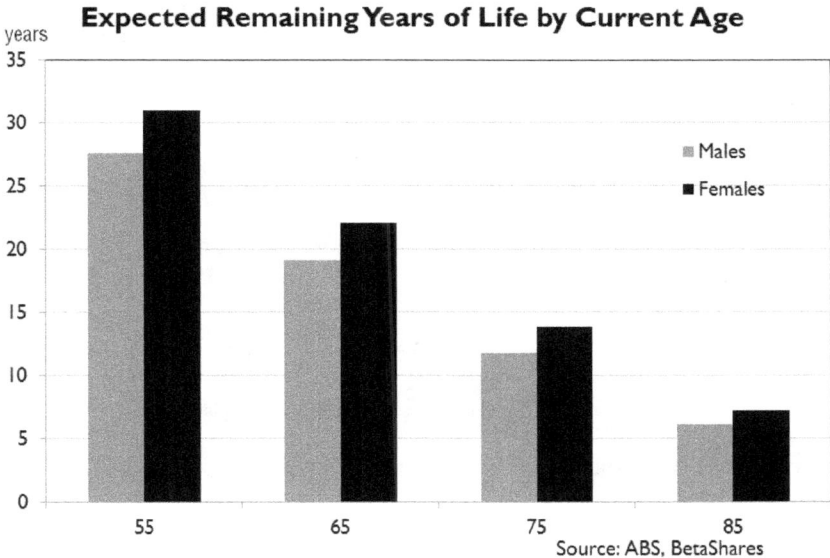

Source: ABS, BetaShares

ACHIEVING RELIABLE INVESTMENT RETURNS REMAINS DIFFICULT

The sobering reality for those facing retirement is that risk markets remain just as volatile as ever. Indeed, history suggests the Australian equity market can suffer a 30-50% total return decline at least once every 10-20 years. The great crash of 2008 – which likely still lingers in many reader's memories – was one of the worst on record. And this was a period in which the Australian economy avoided a recession!

Based on current life expectancy estimates, therefore, those entering retirement can expect to face at least one more gut-wrenching market decline in their lifetime.

All Ordinaries Draw Down Curve*: 1871-2015
return index, end of month data

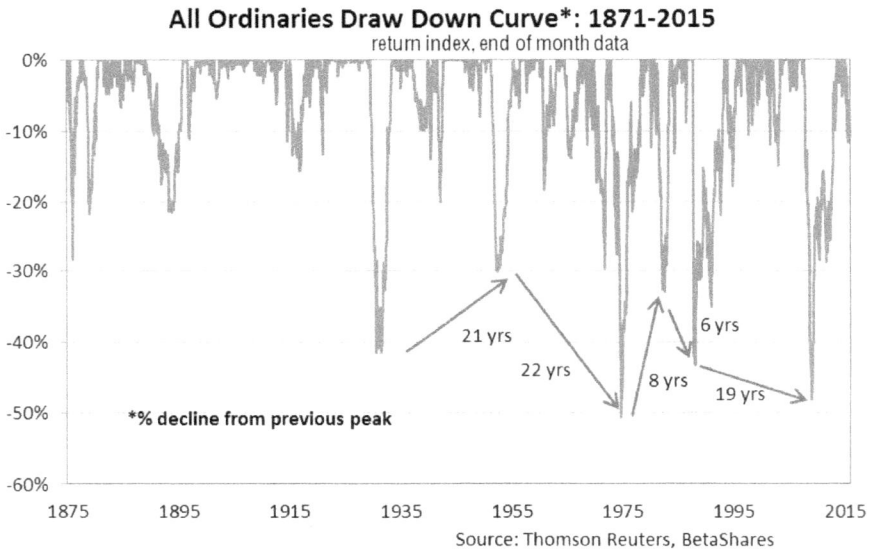

Source: Thomson Reuters, BetaShares

Of course, those nearing retirement can avoid these risks by seeking the safety of less volatile asset classes, such as cash and bonds. But here's the problem: returns from safer assets have collapsed in recent years. The real (inflation-adjusted) returns provided by cash have fallen from just under 4% as recently as the 1990s, to just under 2% this decade. The real yield on long-term government bonds – which provides the basis for most fixed income funds – has declined from around 5% in the 1990s to only 2% this decade. This means investors need to sacrifice a lot more in forgone returns to reduce portfolio volatility.

Australian Cash and Bond Real Yields*

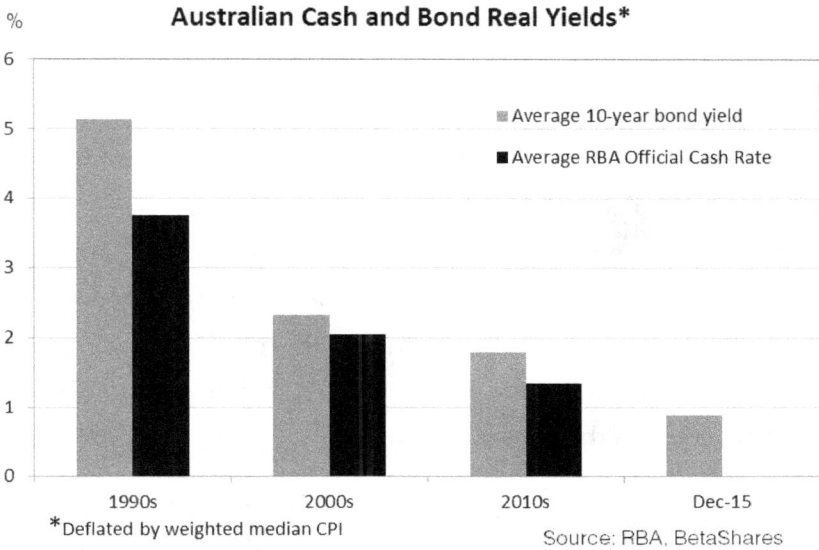

%

- Average 10-year bond yield
- Average RBA Official Cash Rate

1990s   2000s   2010s   Dec-15

*Deflated by weighted median CPI

Source: RBA, BetaShares

As of December 2015, underlying inflation was running at around 2% - equal to the RBA's official cash rate, implying a zero *real* cash rate.   Australian 10-year government bonds yields were only 2.85%, implying a real bond yield of just under 1%.

What's more, with many expecting long-term interest rates to rise slightly in coming years (to around long-term average levels), the medium-term return on bonds bought today is likely to be even lower than today's low yields - due to expected capital losses. Depending on how high interest rates eventually rise, bonds are not currently the safe haven that many asset allocation strategies typically assume.

PENSIONS AND SUPER CONCESSIONS COULD BE CUT

Not only is our ability to provide for our retirement being challenged by our lengthening life span (which, of course, is a good thing!), and troublesome trends in investment markets, but the safety net of publically provided pensions and the generosity of super concessions could also be vulnerable to future government policy changes.

Due to pressure on tax revenues and weak recent economic growth, the Australian Federal Government is still running a large budget deficit – which is proving difficult to reduce. In the longer-term, pressure on the budget will grow as our ageing population generates increased pension and health care costs. Population ageing also means fewer workers will be left to pay the taxes necessary to fund these public benefits.

According to Federal Treasury projections, Government spending on pensions will rise from 2.7% to 3.7% of gross domestic product (GDP) over the next 50 years, an increase of approximately $16 billion in today's dollars. Spending on health care will rise even more – from 4.1% to 7.0% of the economy. There will also be increased spending on aged care and disability support at the State Government level.

Federal/State Government Spending Projections

% of GDP

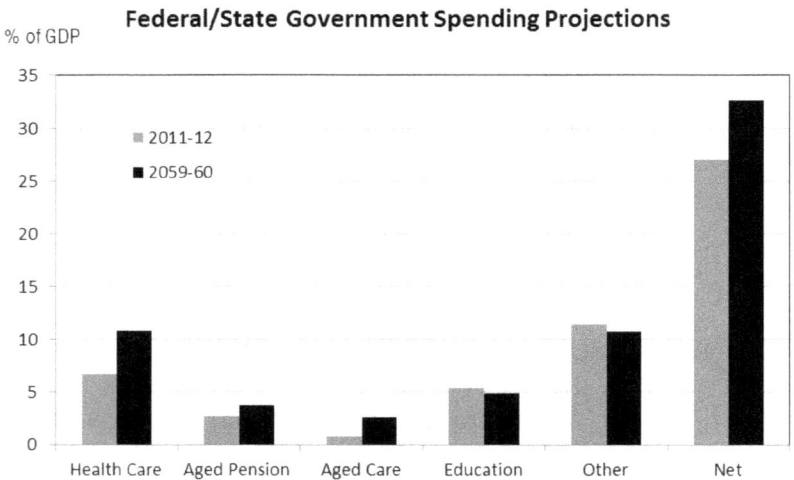

Source: Productivity Commission

All total, the net increase in Federal and State government spending commitments due to the population ageing (i.e. even *after* adjusting for some cuts in spending on education) is equal to 5.8% of GDP, or $93 billion in today's dollars – an increase which must be met each and every year.

Give this ageing demographic outlook, the Government's ability to provide pensions and other retirement concessions in coming decades will be challenged.   The pension benefits that current retirees enjoy could well be cut back in coming years, as might the still considerable tax benefits associated with savings through superannuation.

RUNNING AN *SMSF* CAN BE COSTLY AND COMPLEX

Rightly or wrongly, more and more Australians are choosing to invest for retirement through self-managed super funds (SMSFs).

In the past decade alone, the share of superannuation assets managed by SMSFs has increased from 20% to 30% - surpassing the share of assets managed by either retail or industry funds. As of June 2015, the Australian Tax Office estimates that there were 557,000 SMSFs with just over 1 million members, who collectively hold $590 billion in assets.

Controlling one's own destiny is fair enough. SMSFs are attractive in part because of the relatively greater investment flexibility they offer. Small businesses, for example, can own business assets – including their commercial premises – through their SMSF and obtain concessional tax benefits. It's also still possible for SMSFs to

undertake limited recourse borrowing[3] to purchase other assets –
residential properties are particularly popular in this regard.

Given how fund managers lost significant amounts of money
during the global financial crisis, many investors appear to have
decided they can do better on their own – and possibly save on
investment management fees in the process.

That said, running an SMSF does present numerous challenges. It
involves more administrative effort than simply giving your money
to a retail or industry superannuated fund to invest on your behalf.

A study conducted for the Australian Securities and Investments
Commission (ASIC) by Rice Warner Actuaries[4] found that, on
average, SMSFs which outsourced all administration costs (which is
a fairer comparison to retail and industry super funds that also do
that for you) faced total costs in 2013 of approximately $4,500. This
amount did not vary greatly with fund size.

As seen in the chart below, as retail and industry super funds
typically charge a fixed percentage of funds under management,
they tend to have lower costs for fund balances up to around
$300,000. Industry super funds, however, were cheaper still, and
tended to have lower costs for all fund balances as high as $500,000.

This means that relatively small SMSFs face onerously high costs (to
run their funds) as a percentage of their funds. If your fund is only
$50,000, for example, and your running costs are $5000 – then you

---

[3] In the event of loan default, lenders only have claim to those SMSF assets
purchased with the borrowed funds.
[4] *Costs of Operating SMSFs*, Rice Warner Actuaries, May 2013.

are paying management fees equal to 10% of your fund each and every year!   Your investment returns would have to be pretty spectacular to get ahead after giving up almost 10% of your SMSF fund each year simply to pay fees.

Superannuation Administrative/Investment Costs

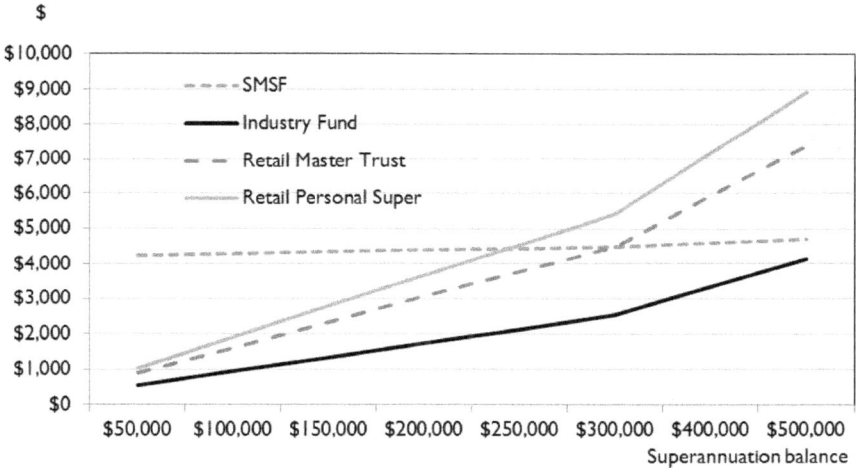

$

$10,000	
$9,000	- - - -SMSF
$8,000	——Industry Fund
$7,000	— — Retail Master Trust
$6,000	——Retail Personal Super
$5,000	
$4,000	
$3,000	
$2,000	
$1,000	
$0	

$50,000 $100,000 $150,000 $200,000 $250,000 $300,000 $400,000 $500,000

Superannuation balance

Source: Rice Walker

Against this, as seen in the chart below, many industry super funds will charge only around 1% of your funds each year to run your super – including providing accounting and investment advice. As an SMSF, even if you invested in direct shares only, and only paid $2000 a year to run your fund (half the average), you'd still need at least $200,000 in funds under management for your management fee to not exceed the 1% charged by a typical industry super fund.

Superannuation Administrative/Investment Costs

% of funds

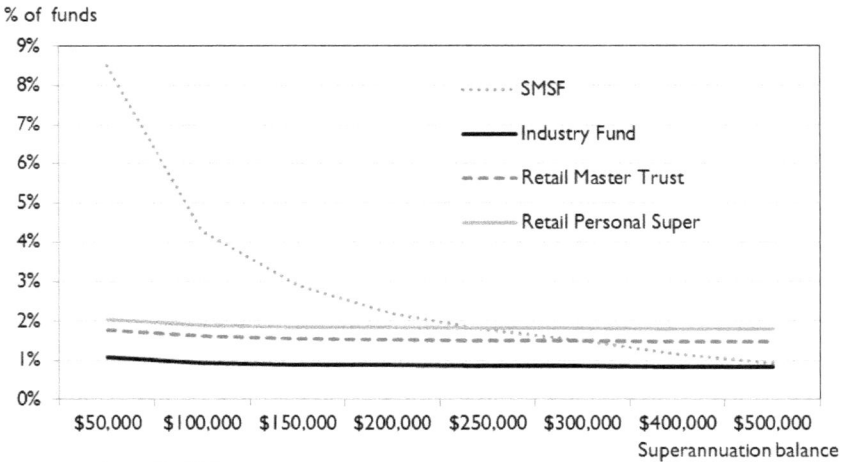

Source: Rice Walker

Sadly, evidence suggests many Australians don't make these comparisons. Indeed, according to data from the Australian Tax Office's 2013-14 SMSF Statistical Overview Report, approximately 65% of SMSF members had balances of less than $500,000. Average operating expense ratios for balances below this size were at least 2%, and for the almost 10% of SMSF members with a balance of less than $50,000, operating expenses averaged 10%!

It's no surprise that in recent years at least, the smaller the SMSF fund, the poorer the return. According to the ATO, the average annual return in the five years period ending in 2013-14 for SMSF funds with less than $50,000 in assets was *minus* 13.1 percent. On the other hand, those with more than $2 million in assets enjoyed an average gain of 8.6%.

SMSF Size, Costs & Performance Review			
Fund size	% of SMSF members*	Operating Expense Ratio**	Return on Assets**
> $0-$50k	8.6%	10.0%	-13.1%
>$50k-$100k	9.7%	5.0%	-4.1%
>$100k-$200k	16.9%	3.7%	0.2%
>$200k-$500k	30.6%	1.9%	4.0%
>$500k-$1m	19.3%	1.0%	6.1%
>$1m-$2m	10.4%	0.7%	7.2%
>$2m	4.6%	0.4%	8.6%

Source: ATO *2013-14 **Average for 5-yrs to 2013-14.

Note over this period, industry and retail super funds regulated by the Australian Prudential Regulation Authority (APRA) enjoyed an average annual return on assets of 8.7% - compared with an average across all SMSFs of 7.2%. As we'll see below, SMSFs tend to be cash heavy – which allowed them to outperform the average industry or retail super fund return during the global financial crisis. However, this has also meant that they've tended to underperform during the post-GFC equity market rebound.

Of course, there are ways to save costs when running an SMSF. For starters, many SMSFs prefer to directly invest in shares, effectively avoiding fund management fees which can typically take another 1 to 2% from your returns each year.

Evidence also suggests that a large number of SMSF investors are making their own investment decisions, without the help of a financial advisor. According to an industry survey, as of June 2014, approximately 59% of SMSFs are investing without the aid of a financial advisor[5].   Although this saves money, it leaves the responsibility for making sound investment decisions squarely in the hands of SMSF trustees.

Unlike simply leaving your money in a superannuation fund, running an SMSF requires deciding where and how to investment your money yourself – either alone or with the aid of a financial advisor.

In fact, each SMSF is required by the Australian Tax Office to formally document an *Investment Strategy*, detailing how the money is to be invested and why. The document must show that the SMSF trustee has taken into account the risk associated with certain investments, and that they are appropriately considering fund members' financial circumstances and objectives. The strategy must also show that the diversification benefits of investing across numerous different asset classes have been considered – a fund that invests in a single asset (such as a small business premises) could be seen as overly concentrated. The document must also demonstrate that the SMSF is invested in sufficiently liquid assets to pay cash expenses (such as accounting and auditing fees) as they arise.

It's not obvious that all SMSFs are meeting these requirements. Evidence from the Australian Tax Office, for example, suggests the average SMSF fund has a relatively heavy exposure to low-yield cash products, offset by a relatively high exposure to much more volatile individual Australian company shares. While low risk, cash

---

[5] Investment Trends Self-Managed Super Fund Planner Report 2014.

can be a major drag on investment performance. This would not usually be appropriate for younger investors who are still in their capital accumulation phase.

By investing in individual Australian stocks (rather than, say unlisted managed funds, exchange traded funds, or LICs), investors may not be sufficiently diversified against company-specific risks. Indeed, another survey suggested that approximately half of SMSFs used no more than 10 stocks for their Australian share allocation[6].

SMSF Asset Allocation: June 2015

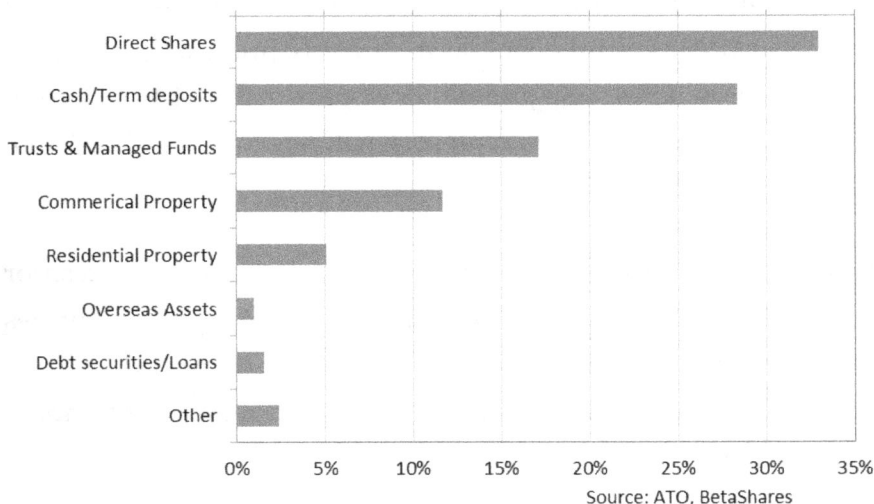

Source: ATO, BetaShares

According to the ATO's survey, SMSFs have a large exposure to commercial property – which likely reflects the tax benefits for small businesses that place their business premises in a SMSF. At the same time, SMSF exposure to international investments is very

---

[6] Multiport June 2013 survey into Australian SMSFs.

limited. All this raises the question of whether SMSF portfolios are appropriately diversified.

Meanwhile, residential property still accounts for less than 5% of SMSF assets. However, this figure has grown strongly in recent years - doubling from 2008 to $21.7 billion in June 2015. Reflecting an easing in borrowing restrictions, limited recourse borrowing has surged from $2.5 billion in June 2012, to $15.6 billion by June 2015.

 The Reserve Bank has expressed concerns that some SMSFs may be getting carried away with property investment and overpaying – which could hurt long-run returns. More broadly, investors should be reminded that over the long-term property prices are unlikely to exceed household income growth, or approximately 4 to 5 percent per year. As we'll see later, this is half the likely return from Australian equities.

In searching for better yields than what is available from cash or bank deposits, SMSFs have also been big buyers of hybrid securities issued by banks which – while high yield – still offer a lower likely total long-run return than bank shares (as they miss out on capital growth), though arguably without much risk reduction.

Most recently issued bank hybrids can be converted into equity capital by regulators – exposing investors to loss – should banks get into financial difficulty and need more equity on their balance sheet. While investors in bank equity will lose out first should a bank get into financial difficulties, investors in hybrids may not be far behind.

To the extent that a large chunk of retirement funds are invested into one's business premises or a handful of Australian stocks, SMSF investors are exposed to major downturns in the commercial property market and/or the market value of certain stocks.

At the other extreme, those seeking safety through a large exposure to cash are sacrificing returns - which then raises the risk of not having enough money to fund a decent retirement.

While running a SMSF offers investors greater flexibility in how to invest money, it is not without considerable costs - caution is still required to ensure that hard-earned retirement money is not squandered.

MANY INVESTORS STILL DON'T USE ETFS

Many SMSF investors and financial planners are avid ETF users. Indeed, according to the latest BetaShares/Investment Trends Survey, there were more than 200,000 ETF investors in late 2015 – a ten-fold increase over the mere 20,000 ETF investors in 2008. Of these, 83,000 – or 41% were SMSF investors – up from only 10,000 SMSF ETF investors in 2008.

What's more, approximately 44% of financial planners say they now recommend ETFs to their clients, which is up from only 15% as recently as 2008.   By late 2015, ETF funds under management amounted to approximately $20 billion.

So far so good, but given the needs of local investors and given international trends, there still appears to be a lot of untapped demand that could and should be filled in coming years.

After all, the total number of ETF investors still accounted for only roughly 3% of the 6.5 million adult Australians that the ASX[7] estimates own some listed investment. These numbers also imply that almost 85% of the more than half a million SMSFs across the country had not yet invested in ETFs.

As of late 2015, 56% of financial planners were still not recommending ETFs to their clients - the latest survey, however, did suggest a further 20% were planning to start recommending ETTs in 2016.

At $20 billion, moreover, ETFS still account for only around 1.3% of the $1.5 trillion market capitalisation of the Australian stock exchange – compared with approximately 3% and 7.5% of the Canadian and United States share market capitalization, respectively.

Of course, one of the hurdles to more rapid take-up of ETFs in Australia is better investor education. Until recently, it has not been in the interest of the largely commission-dependant financial planning industry to recommend products (like ETFs) that pay no up-front or trailing commission.

Similarly, it has also not been in the interests of many in the entrenched funds management industry – which has enjoyed lucrative management fees for often questionable performance – to embrace a product (like ETFs) which often only claim to match market performance, but at a far lower cost. The following section aims to fill some of these gaps in investor knowledge.

---

[7] ASX *Share Ownership Study* 2014.

As we'll see, while some care is still required when investing in ETFs, ETFs also promise many benefits that (sadly) too many Australians are still not aware of.

STEP 2:

Understanding what ETFs are and how to use them

WHAT AM I INVESTING IN? THE THREE KEY FEATURES OF AN ETF

There are three key features to understand about the typical exchange traded fund, or ETF.

For starters, they are *traded on an exchange*, meaning they can be bought or sold on the Australian Securities Exchange (ASX) just like an ordinary company share – such as the Commonwealth Bank (CBA) or BHP-Billiton (BHP). Each ETF has its own unique ASX code that can be used to enter trades via an online or phone broker.

To buy the BetaShares FTSE RAFI Australia 200 ETF, for example, you just enter its code, "QOZ," into your online broker website or quote this code to your stockbroker, choose how many units you wish to buy, and decide whether you will enter a "market price" or a "limit price" order – just as you would for any individual company share.

We'll discuss the specifics of buying ETFs through the ASX later in this book.

Second, ETFs are *managed funds* – they pool money from investors and use the proceeds to buy other financial securities or assets, like shares or bonds. In this sense, ETFs are just like any (unlisted) managed fund that is available from the likes of AMP Capital, Macquarie, or BT Funds Management – only you don't need to fill out complicated forms and mail off cheques to buy fund units. Instead, you buy directly on the ASX.

In fact, ETFs in this sense are like listed investment companies (LICs), which are other investment funds that can also be bought and sold through the ASX. However, ETFs have a unique structure that offers certain advantages over LICs.

The typical ETF, moreover, is an exchange-traded managed *index* fund – which means that it only tries to match the performance of an investment index (such as the S&P/ASX 200 index of the top 200 Australian companies weighted by market capitalisation), rather than try to beat it. In this sense, ETFs are *passive* investments – that can track any number of investment benchmarks covering the local or international equity markets, commodities, cash or bonds.

As we'll see, all these features give ETFs numerous advantages. By trading on the ASX during the day, they are liquid. As a managed fund, they also offer convenient diversification. And by being typically indexed or passive in nature, they are transparent and enjoy low management fees – not to mention tax efficiency by having low turnover.

All that said, it's really the unique structure of ETFs that sets them apart from other exchange-traded or unlisted, active or passive, managed funds. As a result, this structure is worth exploring and understanding in detail.

ETF'S UNIQUE STRUCTURE

This may get a little tricky, but stay with me, because what follows is important to understanding ETFs.

As noted, the key feature to appreciate about ETFs is their unique structure. Traditional managed funds take in money from investors and use the proceeds to buy investments in the market. This means that when many investors in the fund decide to sell, the manager needs to sell some stock to raise cash to meet the redemptions - triggering capital gains taxes for all fund investors.

This traditional approach also means that those funds that choose to list on the market - listed investment companies (LICs) - often trade at prices that don't necessarily reflect the underlying net asset value (NAV) of the investments they hold.

Why? The supply of LIC units readily available on the ASX does not automatically adjust to reflect demand – which would help keep LIC prices close to the underlying net asset value of the shares, bonds, or commodities they invest in. If there is a large sell down in a LIC on a given day, for example, the only way the market will clear is by a large enough price drop to lure in new buyers – and this price may well be below the LIC's NAV.

Managed Funds vs. ETF

Traditional Managed Fund Structure

ETF Structure

As a result, many LICs may often trade at up to 10%-20% or more below their net-asset value.

ETFs, on the other hand, are so-called "open-ended" funds, meaning supply can adjust to demand swings *throughout* the trading day. How so? Each ETF trading on the ASX has one or more dedicated professional traders or market makers (known as authorised participants or "APs") that are employed to make units available for sale or purchase through the trading day. And, uniquely to ETFs, APs have an ability to add to or withdraw from the supply of ETF units by trading directly with the ETF issuer (such as, with BetaShares) at the ETF's net asset value. LIC's don't have this ability.

As a result, should investor ETF demand exceed what is currently available, the APs can simply create more units (issued by the ETF issuer) to meet demand. This is done by buying the underlying assets on the market and bundling them into parcels that match the composition of a specific index or asset class the ETF aims to track (i.e., all 200 stocks in the S&P/ASX 200 index). These parcels are then delivered to the ETF provider who, in exchange, issues the AP with ETF shares which can be on sold on the open market.

Similarly, APs can also soak up supply by buying ETF units on the market and effectively selling them back to the ETF provider at its NAV.

Due to competition between ETF market makers – and their potential to make 'arbitrage profits' in trading ETFs – this process also means the best bid and offer prices quoted for an ETF will typically be close to its NAV.

To see why, consider what would happen if an ETF's current offer price (i.e. the price at which you could buy it on the exchange) was well above the NAV of its underlying securities portfolio. In this case, an ETF market maker could buy up parcels of the underlying securities and exchange them for ETF units with the ETF provider, and the ETF units could then be sold on the market at a profit. This process would continue until the ETF's prices were bid down (and the price of the underlying securities bid up) until this arbitrage profit opportunity was eliminated.

Similarly, if the ETF's offer price was well below the NAV of its underlying securities, the ETF market maker could then buy ETF units on the market and exchange them with the ETF provider for parcels of the underlying securities, which could then be sold on the market at a profit. Again, this process would continue until the price of the ETF was better aligned with the NAV of the underlying securities.

For investors, this structure generates two key benefits. For starters, it means there are no capital gains tax liabilities generated for remaining investors when one group decides to sell out of the fund. That's because when the ETF provider gives back underlying securities to the AP in exchange for redeemed ETF units it is regarded as an "in-specie" transfer of assets that does not generate capital gains.

The second important benefit is that this structure means that ETF market prices should track the NAV of the underlying securities or assets (i.e. shares, bonds, or commodities) quite closely. If the S&P/ASX 200 index rose 5 per cent in a week, for example, then an ETF which tracks this index would rise by virtually the same amount (before any fees and expenses).

The chart below shows that the difference in one year returns from the STW ETF (an ETF which aims to track the S&P/ASX 200 Index) and the S&P/ASX 200 benchmark is usually within one tenth of a percentage point.

The same thing can't be said for LICs. If the market value of the shares they own rose 5% in a week, there's no guarantee the LIC's market price would rise to a similar degree. Instead, as noted above, many LICs often trade at substantial discounts or premiums to net asset value.

Tracking Error for State Street's STW

Annual per cent change

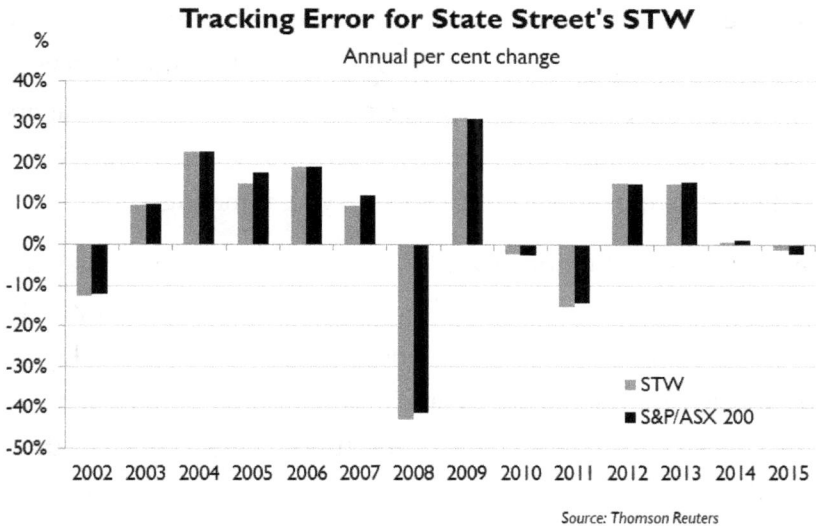

Source: Thomson Reuters

Aside from this unique structure, the other advantages of ETFs are similar to those of index investment funds: transparency, simplicity, and relative cheapness – often without sacrificing investment returns.

OTHER ETF BENEFITS

Let's explore these additional ETF benefits in more detail.

COST

As passively managed funds, ETFs tend to be cost-effective – especially compared with the multitude of actively managed funds – either unlisted or listed - that try to "beat" their respective investment benchmarks over time. Paying more for higher returns is fair enough, but finding an active fund manager that consistently beats the market is not always easy. According to annual surveys conducted by Mercer Research, Australian equity fund managers have, on average, beaten the market by only approximately 1% per year, which is barely enough to cover the typical management fee.

Regular surveys by Standard and Poor's, moreover, find that the vast majority of actively managed Australian funds usually fail to beat their respective investment benchmarks over a several year period. In the 5-years ending in 2015, for example, 67% of actively managed Australian large cap equity funds failed to beat their benchmark.

% of Active Funds that Outperformed their Index

As at 31 Dec, 2015

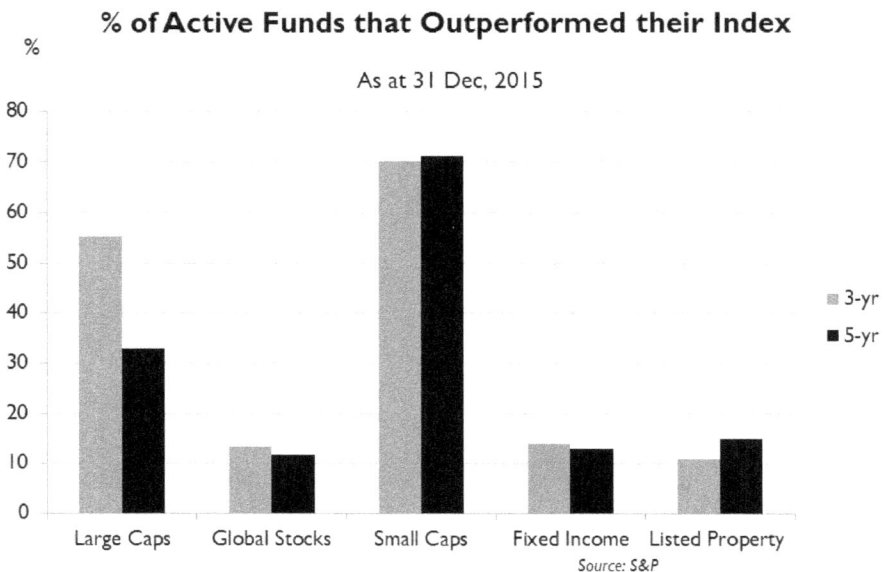

Source: S&P

The exception appears to be small cap funds, which likely reflects the fact that information about the multitude of small listed firms is less widely known in the market - and less likely to be quickly reflected in market prices. For well-known large cap stocks - and fixed income - the market could, however, be considered close to truly "efficient," meaning that all relevant information is quickly reflected in market prices and virtually no group of investors can consistently beat the market.

It also doesn't help active fund managers to outperform when they own such a large share of the market. According to ownership data from the Australian Financial Accounts, household direct holdings of listed shares account for less than 20% of market capitalisation, meaning local and international fund managers *each* own approximately 40% of the market. In the fixed income area, virtually all outstanding government and corporate bonds are held by fund managers, rather than directly by households.

Since fund managers "are" essentially the market, it's impossible for everybody to beat everybody else all the time.

By not hiring expensive analysts and stock pickers in an attempt to beat the market, ETFs are usually much cheaper to run than actively managed retail funds - and charge lower fees accordingly. ETF management fees are usually less than 1%, and often less than 0.5%, compared with an average of approximately 1.5 to 2.5% for many actively managed retail funds.

As with ordinary shares, there is share trading brokerage involved in buying and selling ETFs on the ASX. But ETF providers don't charge entry or exit fees, and there are no trailing commissions paid to financial planners that might recommend them to their clients. Of course, ETFs bought through a financial planner and then held on the planner's investment "platform" might still attract platform fees, not to mention investment management fees that might be charged by the planner. These, however, are not costs charged by the ETF – rather they are charged by the planning service being used.

It remains the case that if your bought ETFs and simply held them long-term in a share trading account, no holding fees – other than those management costs charged by the ETF provider —would be payable for owning these products. The ASX is effectively a free investment platform! Even for purely passive investors, the saving on management fees from ETF investing could mean that their investment nest eggs would be considerably larger in 10 to 40 years than would otherwise be the case.

For example, let's assume that the long-run after-inflation return from the Australian stock market is around 7.5% per year. As seen in the chart below, this means that a $100,000 investment portfolio that paid a 2% management fee would grow at 5.5% per year, reaching just over $800,000 in today's dollars in 40 years. Not bad.

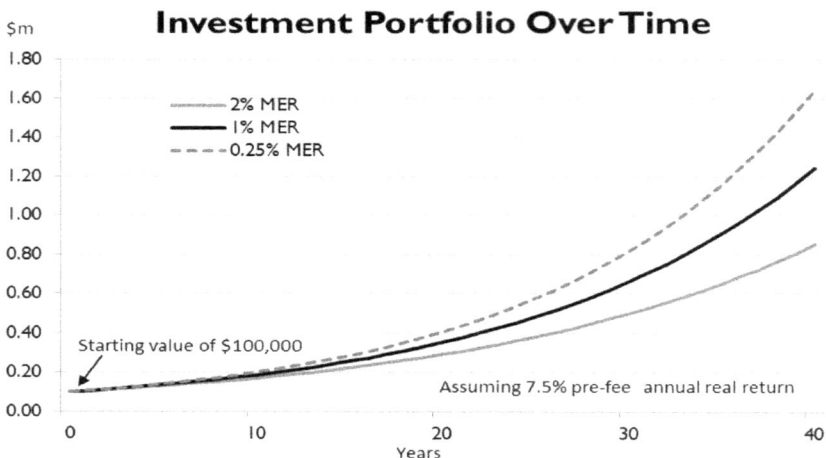

Investment Portfolio Over Time

$m

- ········ 2% MER
- —— 1% MER
- – – – 0.25% MER

Starting value of $100,000

Assuming 7.5% pre-fee annual real return

Years

But, if the investor could shave that management fee to 1%, then the portfolio after 40 years would be worth just over $1.2 million in today's dollars, or approximately 50% more. And if the investor could shave the management fee to a mere 0.25%, the portfolio would be worth a whopping $1.6 million, or twice as much as with a 2% management fee.

In other words, for a $100,000 starting investment, the difference between a fund that charges 2% and one that charges 0.25% is worth a staggering $800,000 in today's dollars over a 40 year period. It's one of the best kept secrets in the Australian financial markets.

DIVERSIFICATION

Many ETFs, like typical managed funds, offer the benefit of easy diversification. Buying only one company share means that investors have a considerable risk tied up in the fortunes of one company. To diversify this risk, investors might instead buy a collection of different company shares in different industry sectors – such as the Commonwealth Bank, BHP-Billiton, Woolworths, and Westfield.

However, to get *real* diversification – so that one's portfolio rises and falls in line with the broader market – might require the purchase of at least 10 to 15 large cap companies. That involves a lot of paper work, not to mention some expertise to ensure that you have a broadly diverse range of company shares. You also have to watch your shares carefully in case any one company falls on hard times and its value starts to plummet.

That's where managed funds come in. Through buying a managed fund, investors get exposure to a broader range of company shares in a single purchase. As an index managed fund, ETFs offer this diversification and the benefit of less paperwork. The only difference from an unlisted index fund is that ETFs are traded on the ASX. As a result, they can be easily bought and sold on the ASX like a company share, instead of having to fill out forms and send cheques to a fund manager.

The SPDR S&P/ASX 200 ETF (ASX Code STW), for example, allows investors to get exposure to Australia's top 200 stocks in one transaction, without having to juggle the investments – and the paper work – of many different stocks.

LIQUIDITY

Unlike an unlisted managed fund, ETFs also offer the flexibility and liquidity of a listed stock. Investors can access all or part of their ETF investments relatively easily by simply selling them back to the market through either their online or phone broker. In this regard, ETFs are similar to listed investment companies, or LICs.

FAIR VALUE

As noted above, unlike LICs, ETF market makers are able to effectively buy and sell ETFs *each trading day* at their respective NAV with the relevant ETF provider so as to keep supply and demand for units in alignment. That means ETFs usually trade at close to their fair value NAV, whereas LICs can often trade at substantial premiums or discounts to NAV.

ASSET BACKING SECURITY

ETFs are effectively "IOUs" – pieces of paper which promise their owners returns in line with a certain investment benchmark. Investors are also able to sell back these ETFs in exchange for the cash equivalent to the market value of the index or asset class being tracked.

But, what happens if the ETF provider goes bust? Do investors have any means to get their money back? Put simply, the answer is a resounding yes!

ETF providers use the funds invested in them to buy the underlying securities that make up the index they seek to track.   These securities, in turn, are held in trust for investors – typically by an independent 3rd party custodian – in an account separated from the ETF provider's balance sheet.   This means that if anything goes wrong with the ETF provider (like insolvency), the assets owned by the Fund are separate, and can either continue to be managed on behalf of investors once a replacement manager is appointed or, in the event the Fund is wound up, the assets are sold and the cash proceeds then duly returned to investors. What's more, other ETF-like structures provide other forms of investor protection.

TAX ADVANTAGES

ETFs also offer tax advantages. As seen in the chart below, ETFs that act like traditional index funds usually have much lower stock turnover than many actively managed funds. As a result, they create less capital gains tax liability for investors within the current financial year.

Portfolio Turnover Rates

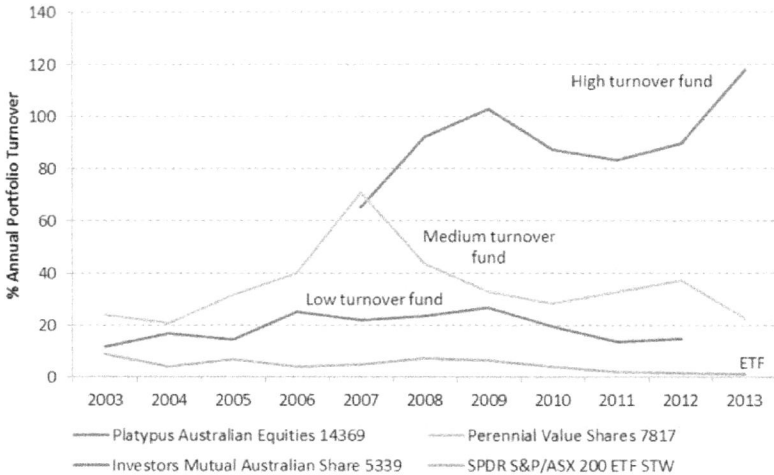

Source: Mercer

In the search for that elusive "hot stock," active managers turn over a significant portion of their portfolio – generating capital gains tax payable for investors on every profitable sale.

As noted above, a second tax benefit is that ETFs are uniquely structured so that investor redemptions create _reduced tax liabilitie_s for the remaining investors compared with typical managed funds. If an investor decides to sell out of a large traditionally constructed managed fund, the fund will need to sell part of its portfolio to meet the cash repayment - triggering a capital gains event for the fund and all its investors for the financial year.

An investor selling down their ETF holding, by contrast, does not necessarily trigger any sale of underlying securities by the ETF provider. Small sales by ETF investors will likely be met out of the trading inventory of ETF units held by APs, as part of day-to-day market trading. If a large investor sells down their ETF holdings, however, it could be facilitated by an AP buying those ETF units for cash and redeeming them for underlying securities held by the ETF provider. The AP could then sell those securities back into the market and recoup their cash.

It is important that this transfer of securities from the ETF provider to the AP is usually done to minimise the capital gains tax obligations for remaining ETF fund investors. This is because the ETF provider is allowed under tax office legislation to identify and allocate much of the capital gains tax liability arising from the sale of these securities to the AP. APs don't mind, since they are considered professional traders and can't benefit from tax concessions on capital gains taxes. APs actually pay no capital gains tax, since all gains on investments are treated as ordinary income and taxed as such in the year in which the gains are made.

Some traditional managed funds also have rules to allocate the capital gains associated with single large investor redemptions to the redeeming investor. However, this is not feasible for smaller redemptions. So in periods when there are lots of small redemptions (e.g., during market crashes), the tax advantage of the ETF structure over that of traditional managed funds is evident.

The generally greater ability of ETFs to protect the remaining investors from capital gains liability arising from redemptions by other investors can become especially important during market downturns – when investor redemptions, large and small, tend to be relatively high. During the global financial crisis, for example, many investors found that they were hit not only with reduced returns, but also with realised capital gains tax liabilities, due to the need for their funds to sell securities to meet the cash requirement of redeeming investors.

TRANSPARENCY

ETFs are also highly transparent. Investors can see the underlying stocks, bonds, or commodities in which the fund is invested – simply by referring to the ETF provider's website. That is often not the case for stocks held by active fund managers, where disclosure is often only made annually, bi-annually, or quarterly. As the ASX-traded funds market evolves, however, and more actively managed funds are placed on the market the frequency with which underlying investments can be reviewed will likely become more restricted.

Only recently, Magellan Financial Group brought to the market actively managed funds that are similarly structured to an ETF, such that market prices should track the fund NAV reasonably closely – unlike in traditional LICs. That said, so as to protect its investment strategies, Magellan is only required to disclose which investments are in the ASX-traded fund on a quarterly basis (and with a several weeks delay).

However, for ETFs, investors can see exactly what the fund is invested in on a *daily* basis.

SURVIVORSHIP BIAS

Unlike the strategy of holding a handful of stocks yourself over the long-term, an underappreciated benefit of passively managed funds, like ETFs, is that they can benefit from survivorship bias. ETFs that track a capitalisation-weighted index of stocks, for example, automatically cut stocks losing significant market value (dropping out of their index), and include stocks gaining market value and entering the index. In this way, although still largely passive in nature, the ETF is effectively cutting poorly performing stocks over time, and replacing them with up and comers making it into the "big league."

ETF CONCERNS/TRADING TIPS

We now know what ETFs are and understand some of their advantages. The next step is to know their risks and complicating factors, as well as the correct way to buy them on the market.

ETFS, ETPS, ETCS, AND EXCHANGE TRADED MANAGED FUND

The first issue is to appreciate that there are numerous variations on the typical ETF structure, each offering their own unique risks and benefits. Some exchange-traded investment products may look and sound like an ETF, but are structured differently – so it's a case of buyers being clear on exactly what they are buying.

To protect investors from confusion, the Australian Securities and Investments Commission (ASIC) has set strict labelling guidelines on ETF-type products traded on the Australian Securities Exchange (ASX).

At the broadest level, we have exchange traded products (ETPs), which encompass classic exchange traded funds (ETFs), as well as *structured products* and *managed funds*.

Exchange Trade Products

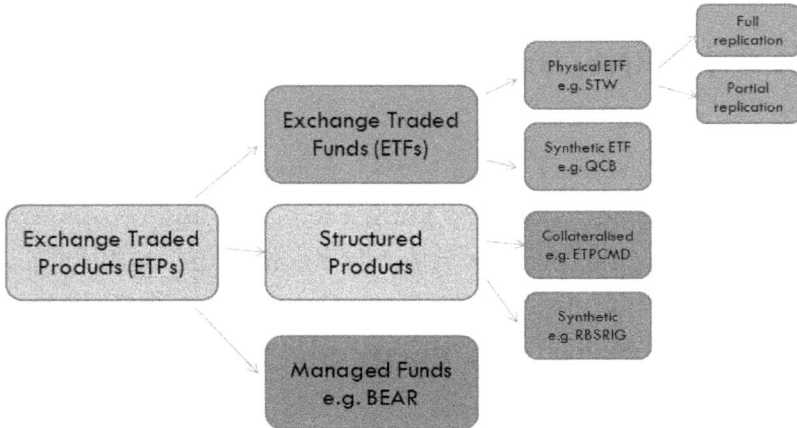

ETFs

ETFs are the easiest and most transparent products to understand. They remain, by far, the most popular ETP product in Australia. ETFs must be run as a managed investment scheme (MIS), and involve collective ownership of a pool of assets held in trust by ETF providers on behalf of investors.

ETFs can be physical or synthetic. *Physical ETFs* are by far the most common in Australia, and seek to match index returns by owning the underlying physical securities (i.e., company shares or bonds) that make up an index – either fully (full replication) or by a representative sample (optimal replication). A physical ETF that sought to match the returns of the S&P/ASX 200 equity index, for example, would own all 200 Australian listed company stocks that are part of the index in proportion to each stock's market capitalisation weight.

Synthetic ETFs, by contrast, are usually created when it is not possible for the fund manager to physically own the underlying asset it is offering exposure to. In these cases, synthetic Australian ETFs place some or all of their funds in cash and contract a third party (i.e., an investment bank trading unit) to vary this cash holding in line with returns from the specific investment index over time. For example, if an index rose 5% in one day, the cash balance held for the ETF would increase 5% - in parallel, it would be reduced 5% if the index fell that amount.

This is accomplished by a contractual agreement between the two parties (known as a "swap") in exchange for a negotiated fee.

Synthetic ETFs are most popular when trying to track commodities that cannot be held and stored physically. For example, a commodity ETF which is seeking to track the performance of crude oil can obviously not physically hold barrels of oil!

Instead, the ETF may seek to match the return performance of a futures contract linked to the commodity's spot price, and to engage a third party to deliver returns in line with this futures contract over time.

Since they rely, at least partially, on derivatives to achieve investment performance, synthetic ETFs have greater "counterparty" risk than physical ETFs – i.e., there is some risk of not getting all your money back if the contracted third party goes broke. However, as we'll see, it's important not to overstate this risk as the media and other uninformed parties often do, as these ETFs are still 100% cash backed (meaning investors have claim to this cash in a stress event). They also have special investor protections set out by the ASX.

Structured Products

The second type of exchange traded product is called a *structured product*. These products, similar to an ETF, can also offer index-like returns. They are similar to synthetic ETFs since they may also rely on contractual arrangements (derivatives) to achieve investment performance.

However, unlike synthetic ETFs, structured products do not need to be run as a managed investment scheme or MIS, which pools all investor funds.   Instead, a structured product constitutes a direct derivative contractual agreement between the end-investor (you) and the structured product provider. In other words, rather than the investor necessarily having an interest in a specific set of assets, they rely on the contractual obligation of the structured product provider to provide returns that match changes in a specified index.

There are two types of structured products. "Collateralised" structured products must provide 100% asset backing, usually in the form of a cash account, which is revalued daily to reflect changes in the index being tracked. That means should anything go wrong, the investor should at least be able to re-claim the cash underpinning the investment deal. In this regard, they are structured somewhat similarly to synthetic ETFs described above.

By contrast, a "synthetic" structured product does not need to provide cash backing. With this product, investors must rely on the continuing credit-worthiness of the provider to ensure that they get the value of their investment back. Accordingly, a synthetic structured product entails greater counterparty risk than a collateralised structured product.

Structured product providers are required to label their products as either collateralised or synthetic. However, adding to potential confusion, structured products can also be described as either exchange traded commodities (ETCs) or notes (ETNs). These sound like ETFs, but, as should be apparent, their structure is decidedly different. Investors who may be concerned about the risks involved in structured products and are interested in investing in commodities should make sure that they "read the label" carefully, and seek out ETF structures if they are available.

Managed Funds

The third type of exchange traded products are called managed funds. These products are structure similarly to ETFs, described above, in that they contain the same investor protections. A product is labelled an exchange traded "managed fund" when the product provider is not tracking a published index – usually because the investment strategy is not easily amenable to being 'indexed.' Exchange-traded managed funds run the spectrum between products that involve a low level of manager discretion and are essentially rules based (for example, products that offer short exposure to the Australian market) all the way through to truly 'actively managed' exchange traded products. These types of products can be identified, as they are required to have "(managed fund)" at the end of their name.

It should be evident that each product type carries its own risks and benefits. Synthetic ETFs and structured products are not necessarily bad, since they often provide the only means of gaining exposure to certain markets, like commodities, and may be entirely cash backed.

It's important, however, that investors know exactly what type of product they are buying.

Physical ETFs are the oldest and most transparent ETP structure, and still dominate the Australian landscape. As a result, much of the following discussion will focus on physical ETFs, though we'll also consider other ETP structures that investors should be aware of as the need arises.

TRACKING ERROR

Tracking error occurs when the net asset value (NAV) of an ETF fails to match the performance of its relevant investment benchmark. For example, if the S&P/ASX 200 index rose 10% over a quarter, yet the ETF's NAV rose only 5%, investors would suffer a fairly sizable tracking error of a negative 5%. Large tracking errors add to investment risk and uncertainty, and would undermine the claim of the ETFs to perform better than LICs in tracking NAV over time.

The degree of tracking error depends in part on the liquidity of the underlying investments in the benchmark, and the methods that the ETF provider uses in tracking the benchmark.

As noted above, physical ETFs seek to match a specific index return by owning the underlying physical securities that make up the index – such as, company shares, commodities, or government bonds. *Full replication* physical ETFs do this by owning every security in the index, in proportion to their respective share of the index. As a result, tracking error for full replication physical ETFs is typically very low.

BetaShares NASDAQ 100 ETF (NDQ), for example, has demonstrated a very low tracking error of around 0.1% to 0.5% p.a., on average.

Where full physical replication of an index is complicated by the sheer number of different securities in the index (such as, the MSCI World Index which has close to 2000 constituents), ETF providers often use *partial or "optimised" replication*, where they own a representative sample of securities within the index – so that the index is still reasonably closely followed without excessive trading costs. In these cases, the ETF provider tries to balance the relative costs of tracking error versus trading costs.

As of the end of 2015, *all* ETFs covering the Australian equity or bond market were full-replication ETFs, whereas some international ETFs (such as, those for emerging markets) used partial replication. Along with equity and bond ETFs, the most popular gold bullion products are also full replication physical ETFs, since they are backed by actual gold bullion holdings held in major vaults around the world. Also, the large cash ETF on the ASX (ASX code: AAA) is a physically replicated product that owns actual cash in the bank.

On the whole, the good news is that large, professional ETF providers that use physical replication techniques do a good job of keeping tracking error relatively low – they're able to track relevant investment benchmarks even when they engage in only partial replication.

Another way that ETFs can track the index is via *synthetic replication* – which, involves the ETF provider holding cash in return for the returns of the underlying index they are seeking to track. The mechanism for this is a derivative contract with a third party bank, which in exchange for a negotiated fee, agrees to deliver returns that are identical to the chosen index each day. This also holds for structured products, which use third party derivative agreements to provide index returns over time.

Perhaps surprisingly to some investors, synthetic replication will always result in the *lowest* tracking error, simply because the counterparty is essentially agreeing to deliver the return of the index. As we'll explore later, the broader range of commodity ETPs on the market are either synthetic ETFs or structured products.

SPOT VS. FUTURES PRICES

Due to the cost and impracticability of physical storage, some commodity ETPs – such as for oil and copper – usually gain price exposure by investing in futures contracts, rather than the physical holdings of the commodities they track. Investors should be aware that this is done simply because there is no other practical way to gain exposure to the performance of these commodities. For example, the 'spot oil' price that is quoted on the news regularly is actually un-investable for investors. This is why product providers have created products which track futures contracts as the closest possible investable proxy to the 'spot' price.

The use of futures in this way, however, can give rise to "tracking errors" relative to the underlying spot commodity price that some investors might not fully appreciate. When futures prices trade at a significant premium to spot prices (referred to as contango), for example, the result is that the price performance of these products can lag the spot price of the relevant commodity over time. This is because these futures contracts lose value relative to the spot price as they approach expiry, and need to be sold or "rolled" into new higher priced futures contracts over time. This need to buy futures at a high price and sell them for less when rolling creates a "negative roll" performance drag relative to the spot price. This premium to the spot price also effectively includes the cost that would otherwise be incurred by investors themselves if they were instead to buy the commodity on the spot market today and store it over the period of the futures contract. Investors are usually prepared to pay a premium to lock-in future ownership of the commodity today at a guaranteed price without having to pay (often significant) holding costs.

In short, if you are very bullish on a particular commodity, but the futures market has already priced in substantial spot price gains in coming months, then investing in a commodity ETP that invests in these futures contracts might not generate as much of a return as expected relative to the 'spot price.'

By contrast, however, returns on these products outperform spot prices when the futures market is in "backwardation" – with futures prices trading at a discount to spot prices. In these cases, investors earn extra premiums as product providers sell expiring futures contracts at higher prices than what they were purchased for and buy cheaper nearer-dated contracts instead.

Of course, an ETF tracking an oil futures contract should still be able to track this futures oil price, irrespective of what is happening to the oil spot price. Indeed, BetaShares launched a currency-hedged oil ETF on the ASX back in late 2011. This ETF aims to track the West Texas Intermediate ("WTI") crude oil futures traded on the New York Mercantile Exchange ("NYMEX"). It is worth noting this ETF has tracked this futures price reasonably well so far.

Oil ETF vs Global Oil Prices

Index Dec'06=100

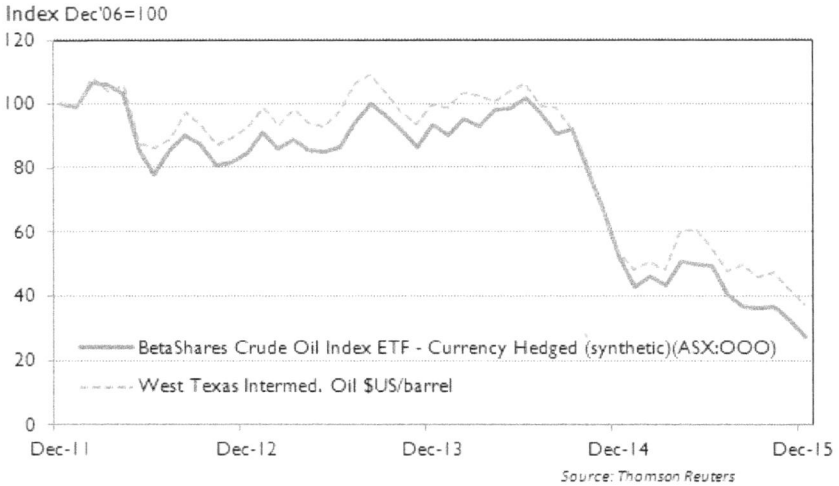

BetaShares Crude Oil Index ETF - Currency Hedged (synthetic)(ASX:OOO)

West Texas Intermed. Oil $US/barrel

Source: Thomson Reuters

ISSUER RISK

Another concern with ETFs relates to issuer risk. What happens if an ETF provider were to go bankrupt - would the investor get back the value of his/her investment?

A key provision in ETF structures (whether physical or synthetic) is that assets held by Fund are held separate from the balance sheet of the ETF provider. That means if an ETF provider were to get into financial trouble, either the Fund would continue with a new provider, or it would be wound up with the assets of the Fund sold and the value of these investments returned to investors.

There is a risk that the value of such investments could fall in the event of a large forced sale. However, this is only a risk when investments are extremely illiquid. In Australia, the major ETF providers are large and well established, and their ETFs generally cover liquid blue chip stocks and bonds.

There's an element of counterparty risk if these ETF providers lend out their security holdings to other professional investors who want to short-sell these stocks (i.e., bet on their prices falling). While this can earn the ETF provider income (and help keep ETF costs down), a problem arises if the borrower gets into financial difficulty and can't give back the stock.

As it stands, most major Australian ETF providers don't engage in stock lending – at least for ETFs that cover the Australian market. Vanguard and BlackRock's iShares do engage in some security lending with their international ETFs, but in these cases there are risk limits on the extent of lending and on borrower quality. Most importantly, borrowers are required to post collateral at least equal in value to that of the securities lent, with these values regularly adjusted to be in line with market prices.   Overall, the risks associated with the failure of an ETF provider should be considered relatively low – since these products are fully backed by underlying securities that can be sold to re-pay investors, if necessary.

COUNTERPARTY RISK

Counterparty risk is the risk associated with the failure of a 'counterparty' involved in constructing an ETP. This risk is primarily associated with synthetic ETFs and structured products. As noted above, synthetic ETFs may pay a third party to provide index returns via a derivative – such as a 'swap' agreement or a futures contract - rather than using the conventional approach of simply owning the underlying securities that make up the benchmark.

As a result, synthetic ETFs can be exposed to risk if the third party derivative provider gets into trouble and is not able to meet their part of the deal.

Counterparty risk is substantially mitigated in Australia due to the way that most ETF issuers construct these synthetic products and, additionally, by rules imposed by the ASX.

The most significant mitigating factor to counterparty risk in Australia is that issuers of synthetic ETFs back 100% of their product with cash. This means that there are actually physical assets underlying the product, which support the value of the investment.

In addition, the ASX has imposed rules regulating the extent of counterparty risk, namely that money owing to the ETF under derivatives (i.e., counterparty exposure) is limited to a maximum of 10% of the ETF's NAV. The ASX also requires that derivative counterparties be of sufficient creditworthiness, being either authorised deposit-taking institutions or foreign banks that meet ASX requirements.

The bottom line is that a minimum of 90% of the value of ASX-traded synthetic ETFs must be backed by either cash or securities which can be used to re-pay investors should the counterparty and/or ETF provider face financial difficulty. Practically, ETF issuers typically manage counterparty risk substantially more conservatively than the 90% limit on a day-to-day basis.

Structured products provide another layer of complexity. As noted above, structured products don't need to be run as managed investment schemes with pooled assets held separate to the product provider's balance sheet. Instead, they are direct contractual relationships between the end investor (you) and the structured product provider.

In these cases, the level of protection afforded to investors depends on the level and quality of collateral assets set aside to protect investors should the structured product provider get into financial difficulty.

Collateralised structured products invest investors' funds in "ring fenced" collateral assets (such as cash), which can reimburse these investors should the provider and/or swap counterparty default on their obligations.   To be labelled "collateralised," a structured product must have full (i.e., 100%) collateral backing, meaning that, in theory, investors should be able to be fully reimbursed through the sale of collateral assets should the structured product provider get into financial difficulty.

As with ETFs, whether investors fully recover their funds, however, depends on the ability to sell collateral assets at close to their presumed market value – which may not be possible in times of financial crisis and/or when markets become illiquid. But, to the extent that collateral assets are cash and highly liquid government bonds, these risks should be fairly small.

Of potentially greater risk for investors are *synthetic structured products*, which don't need to provide "ring fenced" collateral assets, and which leave investors largely reliant on the ongoing solvency of the provider and/or swap counterparty to ensure that they get the value of their investment back when needed.

LIQUIDITY AND BID-OFFER SPREADS

As with ordinary company shares traded on the ASX, there is a difference in the purchase and sale price quoted for ETFs, with this difference known as the "bid-offer" spread. In theory, ETFs should trade close to the NAV and bid-offer spreads should be relatively tight. As noted above, that is because ETFs are structured in a way that arbitrage profit opportunities are opened up for professional authorised traders when ETF prices deviate from their NAV.

This feature provides a major benefit for ETFs and explains why tracking errors over time should be relatively small. It also means that when buying or selling an ETF on any given day, investors should be able to achieve an execution price close to the prevailing NAV. When an ETF is relatively new to the market and has not yet attracted a lot of active traders, there is a risk of buying or selling at prices that deviate notably from NAV. With the right procedures, however, this can be easily avoided.

For example, at any given point in the trading day, the ETF's "market maker" should be offering ETF units for sale or purchase at prices close to - but potentially on either side of - the NAV.

The difference between this bid and the offer price is the "spread" that is earned by the market maker for maintaining a liquid market.

Competition between the market makers should, however, keep these bid-offer spreads relatively narrow. This is exactly how market makers operate when providing prices for any ordinary listed company share on the market.

At any point in time, however, the market maker might only place a relatively small quantity of stock for sale or offer at these best prices.

Should these quantities be bought, the market maker will then quickly replenish the stock available on the market *at the same prices* – provided that the underlying NAV has not changed.

As well as the market maker - and just like with any ordinary share - there may also be other traders that place stock for sale or purchase at less favourable prices. For example, to lock in a profit, a trader might offer to sell an ETF at a price 10 per cent above the current best offer price.

Alternately, a trader might place an order to buy the ETF should prices drop 10 per cent below the current best bid price. All these prices and quantities would be on display through any traditional "market depth" view, such as on an online broker's website.

In this situation, the worst-case scenario for an investor would be to place a "market order" that is large relative to the current quantity on offer by the market maker at the best price. Note, a market order involves asking your broker to buy or sell a fixed number of units at whatever price is needed to "fill" the order. Therefore, if your order is larger than what the market maker is currently offering at the best bid-offer prices, the order will "sweep" over to those quantities on offer at higher prices for purchase, or lower prices for sale.

An investor could then end up with a "bad fill" where they've paid more than necessary to buy ETFs, or received less than they could have when selling an ETF.

Bad fills are sometimes evident when looking at the intra-day high-low price range for certain ETFs – a spike higher or lower in price could mean that an unaware investor has had an order filled at an unfavourable price.

However, this problem is not unique to ETFs. It applies to any (typically small) stock that has a relatively light volume on offer and where a large market order is then placed on the market. Unlike the case for smaller illiquid company stocks, however, ETFs actually have much better liquidity – even if not immediately apparent on the "market depth" trading screen. As we'll see below, a carefully managed order should allow an investor to buy or sell a virtually unlimited amount of ETF units at prices quite close to the NAV.

Where can you find the Intra-Day NAV?

If you are unsure that current market prices reflect the ETF's underlying NAV, this can be checked in numerous ways. Many Australian ETF issuers publish intra-day NAV or 'iNAVs' for their funds. Investors who want to view an ETF's iNAV should refer to the issuer's website – the iNAVs are usually published on these sites. They are otherwise accessible via the ASX by using an ASX ticker. For international ETFs, intra-day NAV quotes are not available as their underlying investments largely trade in offshore markets that may be closed during Australian business hours. iNAVs for international ETFs are often available, however, based on prices from the previous day's trades on an ETF provider's website. During Australian trading time, market makers can still offer international ETFs by hedging their risk through available future markets where possible (i.e., sell US equity futures trading in Asia to hedge a long exposure to the S&P 500 ETF). Due to greater hedging risks, however, bid-offer spreads on international ETFs may be wider – especially when the markets that they cover are not open during the Australian trading day.

Due to the arbitrage process explained above, however, investors can be confident that the fair-value NAV lies somewhere between the best bid and offer prices for these ETFs currently available on the market.

Similarly, the requirement that structured product providers display both bid and offer prices for their products provides an estimate of their "fair value" as somewhere between these prices. Due to competition from other product providers, the bid-offer spread on these products should also not be too wide, so that it doesn't detract from the popularity of the product among investors.

TOP TIPS ON BUYING ETFS

With all this in mind, here are a few other tips on trading ETFs/ETPs on the market.

First, *avoid placing "at-market" buy orders* before the market opens, since it is possible you may get relatively poor pricing. That's because market makers have a hard time pricing an ETF for up to 10 minutes *after* the market has opened, as it takes that long to get valid market prices for all the stocks underlying an ETF. The same holds true near market close. The best time to buy ETFs is when the market is being actively traded in the middle part of most days.

Second, *don't be scared by low 'on screen' volumes* on offer for the sale or purchase of an ETF (such as via an online broker). As noted above, the market maker usually places the best buy/sell prices on offer – the mid-point between these prices should generally reflect the NAV of the securities underpinning the ETF.

If you want to buy/sell a large parcel of one ETF, and the volumes on offer seem low, don't buy/sell them all at once with a large market order, as you could get a poor price (you'll hit the first offer, and then your order will cascade through to higher priced offers until your order is filled).

Instead, one option would be to stagger your purchase/sale by buying/selling what's on offer at the best current market price, and then wait for the market maker to replenish stock on offer near the same market price (provided that the NAV has not changed too much). This strategy, however, involves extra brokerage costs.

Another option is that you could leave limit orders (i.e., a set price) between the bid and offer prices to try and coax a better price from the market maker for the quantity you desire to transact.

If you want to buy, for example, set a limit price order just below the best offer price. If you want to sell, try a price limit order just above the best bid price.

With very large orders (e.g. of more than $100,000), you could even arrange to trade directly with a market maker. You could also ring up your broker directly and arrange a large trade.

You should also note that as an incentive to encourage ETF market liquidity, the ASX offers market makers trading and clearing fee reductions when certain minimum liquidity performance benchmarks - such as average bid-offer spreads - are met.

CURRENCY EXPOSURE

Investors need to be aware that most international equity ETFs on offer in the Australian market are unhedged – meaning that there is not only equity market risk, but also currency risk (for the country/region in which they are investing).

The iShares S&P 500 ETF which trades on the Australian market, for example, moves in line with the $A value of the S&P 500 index. If the US dollar falls, then, if all else is constant, the $A value of this ETF will also fall. It means that investors could miss out if there's a large rally in the US market at the same time that the $A is rising. Similarly, investors could be spared a loss in value if the S&P 500 is falling at the same time that the $A is also falling.

Should one hedge? As a long-term investor, it should not significantly matter provided that the $A does not lose a lot of value over time – which has tended to be the case in recent decades. Shorter-term, there's some evidence to suggest the $A rises and falls in line with global equity markets – suggesting the volatility of global market returns might be dampened somewhat if exposure was left unhedged.

As seen in the chart below, during the global financial crisis, the $A fell as global equity markets fell. It meant that world equities in unhedged $A terms did not fall as sharply as they did in hedged (local currency) terms. Unhedged Australian investors in offshore equities had their $A returns partly insulated by a rise in foreign exchange rates against the $A.

With the rally in equity markets since March 2009, however, world equities did not initially increase as strongly in (unhedged) $A terms as they did on a hedged basis, as the $A also tended to recover.   Over the past few years, however, due to weaker commodity prices, the $A has been falling – even as global markets continued to rise – meaning returns from offshore markets, on an unhedged basis, have been particularly strong.

Global Equity Performance

Index Dec'95 = 100   MSCI World Index

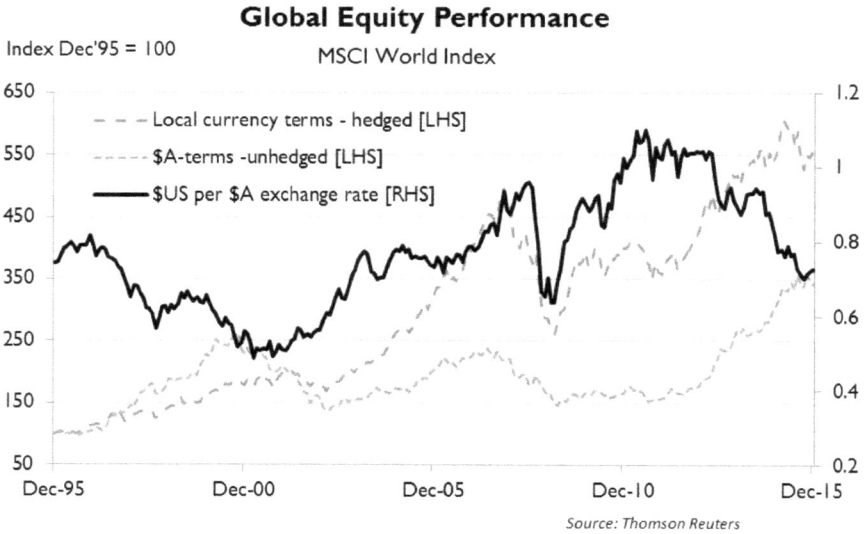

- – – Local currency terms - hedged [LHS]
- ····· $A-terms -unhedged [LHS]
- ──── $US per $A exchange rate [RHS]

Source: Thomson Reuters

It is important to note that distributions are declared and paid by the international ETFs in the relevant foreign currencies. There may be a period of several days, therefore, before they are converted into Australian dollars and subsequently paid to Australian investors. As a result, a major change in the Australian dollar during this period can affect the eventual Australian dollar value of the distribution that is paid.

For those not wanting currency risk, as will be detailed later, there is now a wide range of currency hedged ETFs also trading on the Australian market.

INTERNATIONAL TAXATION

There are also international tax implications that investors need to be aware of. Some international ETFs listed in Australia are cross-listed from the US market, and, as such, a 30% US withholding tax is automatically deducted from their distributions to Australian investors (even if some ETFs include non-US shares).

Investors can, however, fill out a "W8-BEN" form that will automatically reduce this withholding tax to 15%. This form must be completed for each separate cross-listed ETF owned, and a new form needs to be completed for each ETF every three years. While the share registrar sends out the relevant forms to investors after each ETF purchase, the form can also be found on Computershare's website.

You should note that certain government organisations may be subject to zero withholding tax. They must, however, apply directly to the US Internal Revenue Service for this exemption.

Whether or not the W8-BEN form is filled out, investors can receive a tax credit against Australian tax on any withholding taxes paid abroad. Not filling out the form, however, (at least in theory) also legally obligates an investor to complete a US tax return.

Note that the US estate tax may also apply upon the death of an investor who owns an ETF that is cross-listed on the US market. The tax payable, however, may be reduced under the Australian/US estate tax treaty. Certain exemptions may also apply depending on the investor's legal structure.

As will be detailed later, there is now a broader range of international ETFs (including all BetaShares international equity ETFs) that are not cross-listed, but instead are structured as Australian unit trusts/managed funds that invest in international shares. While investors are still subject to US withholding tax, the paperwork requirements to have this tax reduced are undertaken by the ETF provider – investors do not need to fill out a W8-BEN form. Note, moreover, investors in these ETFs are not subject to the US estate tax in the same way they could be with a cross-listed ETF.

In short, international ETFs are subject to more complex tax considerations. This is really only an issue for long-term investors with substantial sums invested in these products. What's more, international ETFs can be structured differently, and investors should compare their relative tax and management fee costs in light of their own specific circumstances.

If you own, or intend to own, a large amount of international ETFs you should consult a specialist tax advisor to know what taxes or special exemptions may apply in your situation.

MARKET PRICING AND INTERNATIONAL TIME ZONES

One last point to note is that when investing in international ETFs we should not expect the day- to-day percentage changes in their price to exactly match the international market index that they seek to track. The reason is that traditional equity and bond markets operate in different time zones around the world, whereas futures markets can trade continuously in a globalised market.

Traders that are making markets in international ETFs during Australia's trading time must base their pricing on what is happening to the price of relevant securities during the current (Asian) trading day (typically reflected in the futures market), not on what might have happened in the US equity market overnight.

For example, if America's S&P 500 index closes up 1% during the US trading session, it does not necessarily mean that an ETF tracking that index (ignoring currency changes) will start

Australia's trading day 1% higher than its closing level from the previous day.

This is because the ASX typically starts trading approximately 4 *hours after* US markets have closed. During this time gap, there could be any number of market sensitive news announcements (such as, a corporate earnings release) which will be reflected in the after-market *futures* price of the S&P 500 index. The prevailing S&P 500 futures price at around the time of the ASX market open will dictate the opening bid and offer prices set by the market markers (as it is, the futures price that traders use to hedge their market positions during the Australian trading day). Similarly, the closing price of the S&P 500 ETF will reflect the S&P 500's futures prices at around market close.

Strictly speaking, therefore, the daily percent change in the ETF's price on the Australian market will reflect the percent change in the S&P 500's futures price at around the ASX market close compared with the previous day's market close. The same broadly holds true for all ETFs/ETPS that track markets which operate in different time zones (to that of Australia).

As should be apparent, the ability of market makers to hedge their positions in international ETPs during the Australian trading day depends in large part on the availability of continuously traded relevant futures price benchmarks. Where these benchmarks are less evident (for example, in emerging markets) the degree of risk faced by these market makers is higher. They compensate for this with somewhat wider bid-offer spreads. As noted above, however, competition between market makers should ensure these bid-offer spreads are no wider than they need to be.

STEP 3:

Knowing what ETFs are available in Australia

———————⌇———————

GLOBAL BACKDROP

ETFs were first traded on the US market in the early 1990s, largely to enable institutional fund managers to better invest the vast sums under their care. US ETP assets have jumped during this 20-year period and now stand at $US2.1 trillion (as of the end of 2015). This is still a relatively small share of the $US13 trillion in total US managed funds.

According to BlackRock Investment, $US2.96 trillion was in global ETP assets by December 2015. That is still a relatively small amount compared with the $US78 trillion estimate of total global funds under management (as of the end of 2014[8]).

Global ETF/ETP Funds Under Management

$USb

As at 30 December, 2015

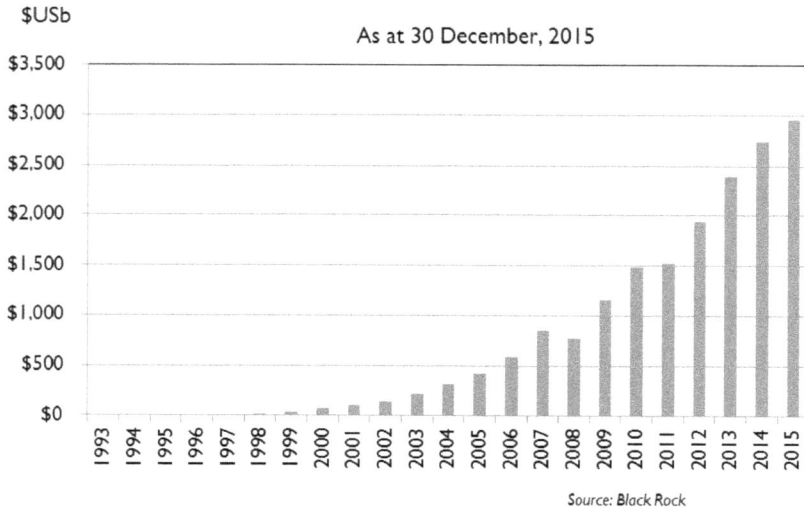

Source: Black Rock

---

[8] PI/Towers Watson Global 500 Research and Ranking for 2014.

The United States accounts for 72% of global ETP assets; Europe accounts for an additional 17%. Asia and Canada account for much of the rest.

Equity ETFs remain the most significant instrument, still making up 80% of the market (as of December 2015). Fixed income and commodity ETFs/ETPs accounted for 17% and 3%, respectively.

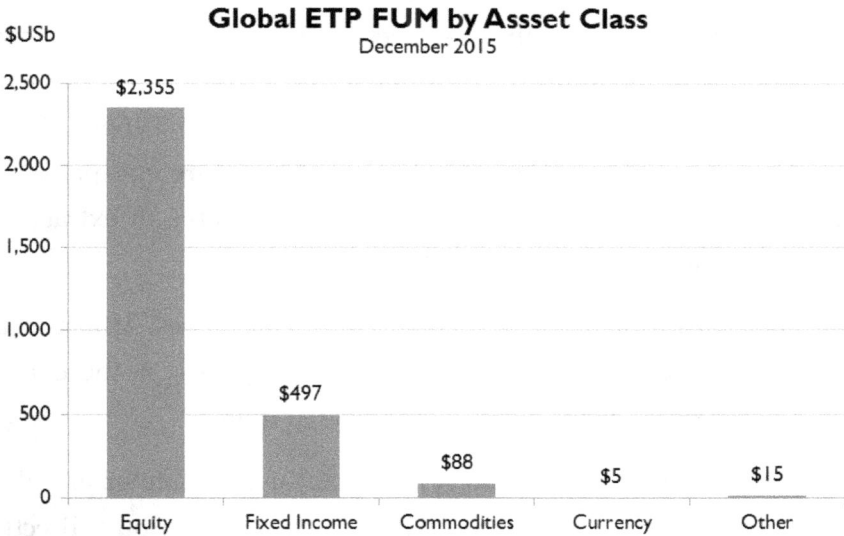

Global ETP FUM by Assset Class
December 2015

$USb

Equity	Fixed Income	Commodities	Currency	Other
$2,355	$497	$88	$5	$15

AUSTRALIAN MARKET OVERVIEW

Australia has been under-served by ETFs for many years, although the situation is rapidly improving. One reason for the slow ETF uptake has been the largely commission-based structure of the financial planning industry – where planners have traditionally earned fees from the investment products they recommend, usually actively managed funds. ETFs are traded on the stock exchange, and like ordinary company shares, provide no commissions to financial planners who recommend them to their clients.

With the move to fee-for-service financial planning, the growth of self-managed superannuated funds, and growing disenchantment with managed funds following their poor performance during the global financial crisis, Australian investor interest in ETFs has been growing. More ETFs are being placed on investment platforms run by planners, meaning that – even though ETFs don't pay commissions – planners can nonetheless still earn investment management fees (to the extent that they are advising their clients about where best to invest). To the extent ETFs are cheaper than most actively managed funds, planners are still able to extract an advisory fee while keeping overall client costs low.

Note that platforms used by planners also charge fees. This means that even platform providers are warming to ETFs, to the extent they can attract more funds invested through them.

Of course, the many investors who do not use a planner are also slowly, but surely, discovering ETPs, which they can buy directly through the ASX on their own.

By December 2015, there were 138 ETPs (comprising ETFs, managed funds and ETNs) listed on the Australian market with a combined market capitalisation of $21.3 billion – a staggering 113% growth compared with December 2013. Growth has been especially strong since the global financial crisis, though ETPs still account for only around 1% of the near $2 trillion in consolidated funds under management across Australia.

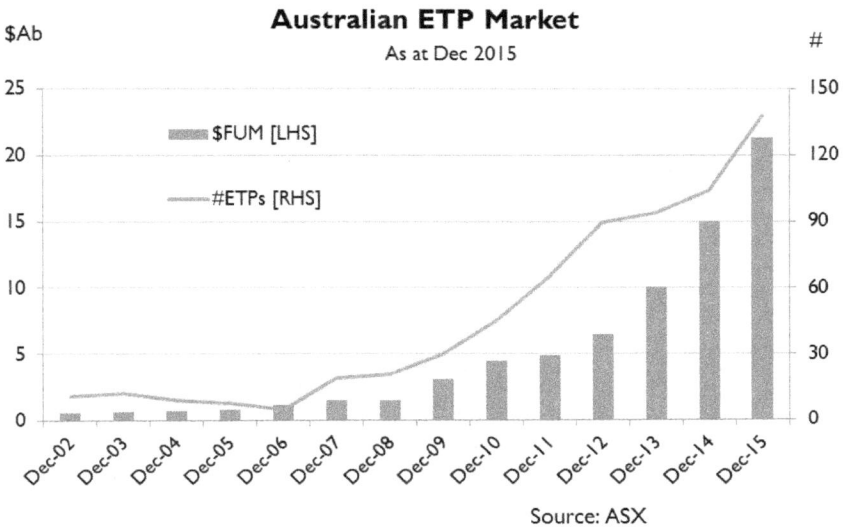

Australian ETP Market
As at Dec 2015

$Ab   #

$FUM [LHS]

#ETPs [RHS]

Source: ASX

Australian equity ETPs account for just under half the market. Among these, broad-based large-cap equity indices account for 63%, "strategy" based equity ETPs (principally with a high dividend focus) account for another 25%, and property ETFs make up another 12%. Industry sector ETFs (for example, finance and resources) and small/mid-cap ETFs have just under 2% of the shares of the Australian equity ETF market each.

The next biggest chunk of the market is accounted for by international equity ETPs, which represent a 40% share. Only recently introduced, cash and fixed income ETPs account for 4% and 5% of the market, respectively, which is still relatively low compared with the 17% of global ETPs invested in these asset classes. Commodity ETPs - largely gold – have a foothold, making up 3% of the local market. Currency ETPs – largely invested in the US dollar – account for 2% of the local ETP market.

Australian ETPs by Asset Class Type, $m
Dec 2015

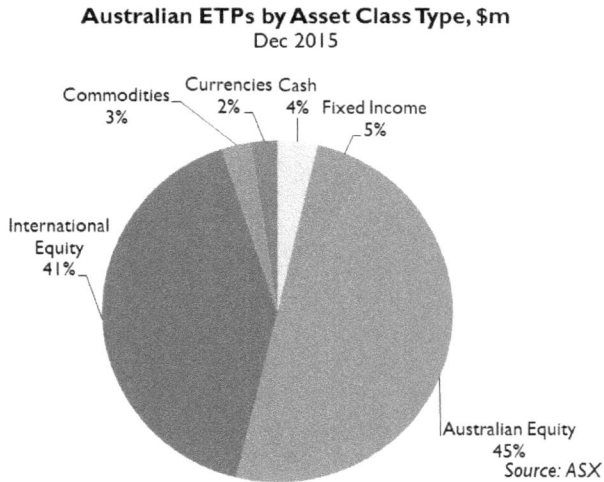

Commodities 3%
Currencies 2%
Cash 4%
Fixed Income 5%
International Equity 41%
Australian Equity 45%
Source: ASX

As seen in the table[9] below, the largest Australian ETP is also the oldest: State Street Global Investor's SPDR S&P/ASX 200 fund, (STW) which tracks the performance of the S&P/ASX 200 index.

Top-10 Australian ETPs by $FUM December 2015 ($m)	ASX Code	ICR*	FUM ($m)
SPDR S&P/ASX 200	STW	0.19	$ 3,202.0
iShares Core S&P 500	IVV	0.07	$ 2,006.6
Vanguard Australian Shares Index ETF	VAS	0.15	$ 1,353.7
iShares S&P Global 100	IOO	0.40	$ 1,062.7
Vanguard US Total Market Shares Index ETF	VTS	0.05	$ 824.2
Betashares Australian High Interest Cash ETF	AAA	0.18	$ 792.8
Vanguard Australian Shares High Yield ETF	VHY	0.25	$ 629.3
iShares S&P Europe	IEU	0.60	$ 627.2
SPDR S&P/ASX 200 Listed Property Fund	SLF	0.40	$ 599.0
Vanguard All-World ex US Shares Index ETF	VEU	0.14	$ 596.8

[9] In the ETP tables that follow through most of this section, ICR* refers to "indirect cost ratio" which includes management fees and some other costs such as administration and custody fees, though not including brokerage costs. All ETPs are listed by alphabetical order of their ASX Code. FUM refers to funds under management. Sources for all tables are the ASX and ETF provider websites.

As of December 2015, STW had $3.2 billion funds under management (FUM). The second largest ETP was the iShares ETP that aims to track the United States' S&P 500 index, and also boasts a very small management expense ratio of only 7 basis points (0.07%).

Popular ETPs include other large cap Australian and international equity products and a listed property ETP, as well as the BetaShares Cash ETF. We'll explore the available ETFs/ETP across each asset class in more detail later.

Reflecting the strong demand for international equity ETFs over the past year, iShares is now Australia's largest ETF provider – having recently overtaken the oldest ETF provider, State Street. The next two largest players are Vanguard and BetaShares. The top four players together account for 90% of the industry's market share.

Australian Top-10 ETP Providers by $FUM December 2015 ($m)	FUM ($m)
iShares	$ 7,196.4
StateStreet	$ 4,923.7
Vanguard	$ 4,747.5
BetaShares	$ 2,285.2
Russell Investments	$ 642.1
Magellan	$ 455.8
ETF Securities	$ 439.1
VanEck Vectors	$ 280.8
UBS	$ 180.8
Perth Mint	$ 79.5

We'll now look specifically at the range of ETFs available within each category.

AUSTRALIAN EQUITY ETFS

LARGE CAP WEIGHTED AUSTRALIAN EQUITY

As seen in the table[10] below, numerous ETFs now provide broad exposure to large cap Australian equities. For the average retail investor, there's not much that separates the traditional market capitalisation weighted ETFs in terms of risk and investment performance - they all cover very similar (even identical) investment benchmarks and are offered by very well-established organisations. Similarities also occur because Australia has one of the world's most concentrated stock markets, with the top few stocks accounting for a relatively large share of market capitalisation.

ASX Code	Product Type	Fund Name	ICR (%p.a.)*	FUM ($m)	# trades	Bid-Offer % spread
\multicolumn{7}{l}{Australian Large Cap Weighted Equity ETPs as at Dec 2015}						
IOZ	ETF	iShares S&P/ASX 200 ETF	0.19	$410.5	890	0.15%
ILC	ETF	iShares S&P/ASX 20	0.24	$306.3	879	0.18%
STW	ETF	SPDR S&P/ASX 200	0.19	$3,202.0	6,421	0.08%
SFY	ETF	SPDR S&P/ASX 50	0.29	$464.1	796	0.07%
VAS	ETF	Vanguard Australian Shares Index ETF	0.15	$1,353.7	3,106	0.15%
VLC	ETF	Vanguard MSCI Australian Large Companies Index ETF	0.20	$55.0	83	0.22%
ZOZI	ETF	ANZ ETFS S&P/ASX 100 ETF	0.24	$1.9	9	0.20%

With $3.2B FUM, State Street's STW covering the S&P/ASX 200 index remains the dominant player in the field.

---

[10] Bid-offer spread refers to the average percent difference in the quoted bid-offer spread during the month of December 2015.

This benchmark covers the top 200 largest and most liquid listed stocks on the Australian equity market - accounting for broadly 80% of the total Australian market capitalisation. In what is an almost identical exposure (and equally priced), iShare's IOZ also covers the S&P/ASX 200 index.

Vanguard's main competing ETF product, VAS, covers the S&P/ASX 300 index which includes the top 300 stocks listed on the market – meaning it effectively covers both "large cap" *and* traditionally defined "small cap" stocks[11]. But given the top 200 stocks accounts for approximately 98% of the S&P/ASX 300 index, this index also tracks the S&P/ASX 200 very closely.

A noteworthy recent entrant into the ETP space is ANZ Bank – the first of the major banks to enter the market. Its broad equity offering tracks the S&P/ASX 100 index.

STW has tended to be the more popular short-term trading tool due to its generally tighter bid-offer spreads, though even here VAS's average spread now appears comparable.

It is important to note that investors also have a choice of investing in only the very largest cap stocks, as covered by the S&P/ASX 20 (iShares), the S&P/ASX 50 (State Street), or the MSCI Large Companies Index (Vanguard) which comprises the top 30 stocks. Note that even the S&P/ASX 20 index, however, accounts for almost 70% of the S&P/ASX 200 index - so these indices tend to correlate fairly closely with broader indices.

---

11 On the ASX, "small caps" are traditionally defined as the smallest 200 stocks by market capitalisation among the top 300 stocks by market cap.

Index share of the **S&P/ASX 300**

%

As at 31 Dec, 2013

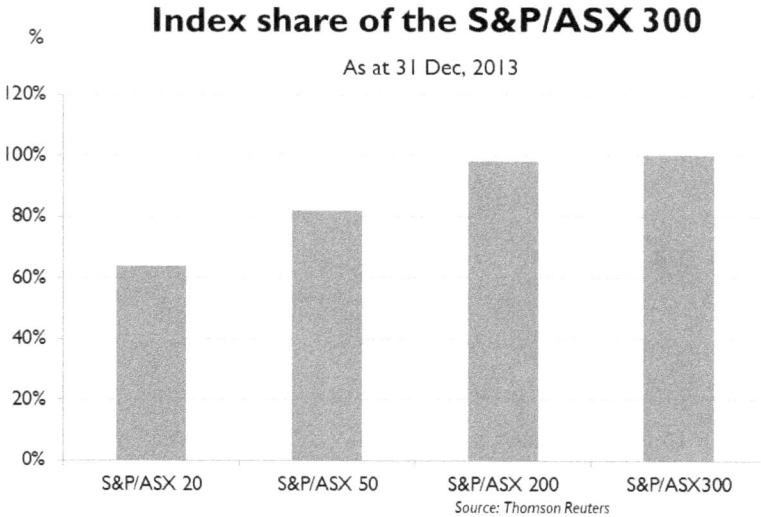

Source: Thomson Reuters

For practical purposes, there's not much difference in investment performance for the average investor.

As seen in the chart below, annualised performance across the major large cap investment benchmarks has been fairly close in recent years – all suffered a large decline during the 2008 global financial crisis. Overall volatility in annual returns is also similar, though with a slight bias to less volatility for the larger cap indices. Also worth noting is that the broader S&P/ASX 300 index – which includes "small caps" has tended to underperform in recent years. However, it did outperform the S&P/ASX 200 Index in 2015.

Australian Broad Equity Market Benchmarks

%   Annual Total Returns

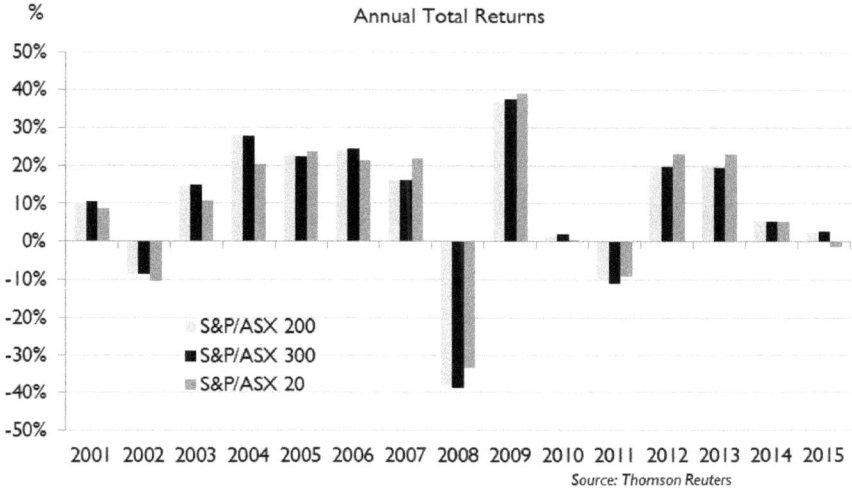

Source: Thomson Reuters

Overall, the Australian market is heavily weighted to finance stocks, with financials, excluding listed property, accounting for around 40% of the S&P/ASX 300 Index, as of the end of 2015. Listed property, which is part of the broader financials sector, accounted for a further 8% of the index, meaning financials overall accounted for almost half the index. The metals and mining sector (a sub-sector of the materials index) accounted for 11% of the index, followed by industrials.

Given the sector breakdown, it's no surprise that banking and mining stocks are among the most important in Australia's broad equity market benchmarks. Australia's top four banks accounted for the top 4 places on the S&P/ASX 200 Index, as of the end of 2015, followed by Telstra and BHP-Billiton.

Compared with major global markets, such as the United States, Australia is overweight in financials and mining stocks and underweight in information technology, consumer stocks, energy, and health care. This should be kept in mind when considering global diversification benefits.

Should the global market enjoy another "tech boom," for example, the local market is likely to be left behind. By contrast, a boom in financial and/or resource stocks should help the local market outperform global peers.

SMALL CAP AUSTRALIAN EQUITY

There are several Australian equity ETFs that focus on the small cap market. iShares, State Street, and Vanguard offer funds that track a passive small caps index, without any attempt to outperform that index.

The challenge with this approach, however, it that Australia's traditional small cap indices include many illiquid stocks and "speculative" mining exploration companies that may never turn a profit. Over recent years, moreover, many active managers in the small caps space have found it relatively easy to outperform these indices by simply avoiding highly speculative resource companies.

The S&P/ASX Small Ordinaries Index is the typical benchmark for this area of the market. The index comprises the smallest 200 stocks among the market's top 300 stocks. Compared with the many hundreds of smaller stocks on the market, this small cap index, therefore, still includes some surprisingly large companies (with an average market cap of more than $1 billion). As shown in the chart below, however, the year-to-year volatility in returns for the small cap index can be notably higher (around one third) than for large cap indices.

Australian Broad Equity Market Benchmarks
Annual Total Returns

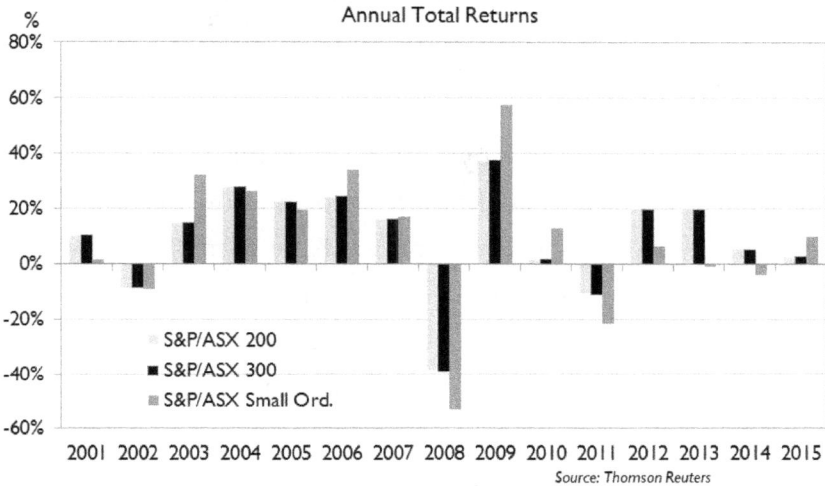

Source: Thomson Reuters

In 2008, for example, the S&P/ASX Small Ordinaries total return index fell 53%, compared with a 38% decline for the S&P/ASX 200 total return index. In 2009, the small cap index rebounded 57% - outperforming the 37% gain for the larger cap index. It's usually the case that the small cap sector falls more in bear markets and rebounds more in bull markets. Over time, however, there's no strong evidence to suggest this sector necessarily outperforms the larger cap sector.

In the 22 years prior to the end of 2015, the S&P/ASX Small Ordinaries sector has produced annualised total returns of 7.2%, compared with 9.9% for the S&P/ASX 200 sector. Small caps have also notably underperformed in recent years, and even posted small losses in 2013 and 2014 compared with gains for the S&P/ASX 200 index. That said, the S&P/ASX 200 Small Ordinaries Index enjoyed an outperformance burst in 2015, as both large cap mining and banking stocks struggled.

Not only has the small cap benchmark struggled to outperform larger cap benchmarks over time, this is also one of the few areas of the market where active fund managers appear to produce consistent benchmark beating returns. As noted above, while regular surveys conducted by Standard & Poor's suggest most active managers can't beat the large cap investment benchmark, around 80% or so of small cap managers have been able to beat the small cap benchmark on a rolling three- and five-year basis. This reflects the far greater diversity of small caps that fund managers can invest in and the greater challenge of market prices readily reflecting all known information about these small stocks.

One apparently easier way to beat the index is to avoid the many smaller speculative mining companies that the index contains. In a sense, the small cap market is less "information efficient," and so more likely to reward stock specific research.

Reflecting this, VanEck Vectors's small cap ETF applies its own filter to weight toward small cap stocks that meet minimum market cap levels, pay a dividend, and generate at least 50% of their earnings in Australia.

ASX Code	Product Type	Fund Name	ICR (%p.a.)*	FUM ($m)	# trades	Bid-Offer % spread
Australian Small/Mid Cap Weighted Equity ETPs as at Dec 2015						
ISO	ETF	iShares S&P/ASX Small Ordinaries	0.55	$33.1	519	0.51%
MVS	ETF	VanEck Vectors Small Cap Dividend Payers ETF	0.49	$33.6	84	0.28%
SSO	ETF	SPDR S&P/ASX 200 Small Ordinaries Fund	0.50	$8.1	40	0.21%
VSO	ETF	Vanguard MSCI Australian Small Companies Index ETF	0.30	$66.4	196	0.33%
KSM	MF	K2 Australian Small Cap Fund (Hedge Fund)	2.00	$26.4	16	n/a

K2 Asset Management's small cap fund is actively managed, and aims to beat traditional small cap benchmarks over time – it does, however, charge a relatively high 2% management fee, and a 20% outperformance fee. That said, since its inception in late 2013 to December 2015, K2's Fund has outperformed the S&P/ASX Small Ordinaries Index.

Although it's actively managed, the K2 Fund is not structured like a traditional listed investment company (LIC), but rather as an exchange traded product or ETP. Unlike a LIC, therefore, the K2 Fund offers regular transparent portfolio disclosure, and the benefit of market values trading closely to the underlying NAV of the securities it holds (i.e., unlike some LICs, the Fund should not trade at a significant discount or premium to net-asset value).

EQUAL OR FUNDAMENTALLY-WEIGHTED AUSTRALIAN EQUITY ETFS

The ETFs mentioned so far track what are known as "market capitalisation" indices, with the weights of each stock typically based on market capitalisation. But, some variations in the traditional "market capitalisation" indexing method have entered the market in recent years.

Australian Large Alternative Weight Equity ETPs as at Dec 2015						
ASX Code	Product Type	Fund Name	ICR (%p.a.)*	FUM ($m)	# trades	Bid-Offer % spread
QOZ	ETF	BetaShares FTSE RAFI Australia 200 ETF	0.40	$87.7	387	0.29%
MVW	ETF	VanEck Vectors Australian Equal Weight ETF	0.35	$75.6	307	0.13%
ETF	ETF	UBS IQ MorningStar Australia Quality ETF	0.30	$55.1	156	0.19%

BetaShares QOZ ETF, for example, is based on a "fundamental indexing" methodology developed by Research Affiliates. Instead of weighting stocks by their market capitalisation – meaning the weight attached to each stock rises or falls in line with its share price - the "RAFI Fundamental Index" invests in the top 200 stocks, as determined by four non-market capitalisation factors: sales, cash flow, dividends, and book value. Simply put, stocks are weighted by each factor, and their average weight across each measure is used as their weight in the index.

Indeed, this methodology has been around for a while and has tended to outperform the S&P/ASX 200 market capitalisation index over time – the same has also been true in the United States. Indeed the 20-year annualised return for the RAFI Australian 200 Index up until the end of 2015 was 11.2%, compared with only 9.0% for the S&P/ASX 200 index.

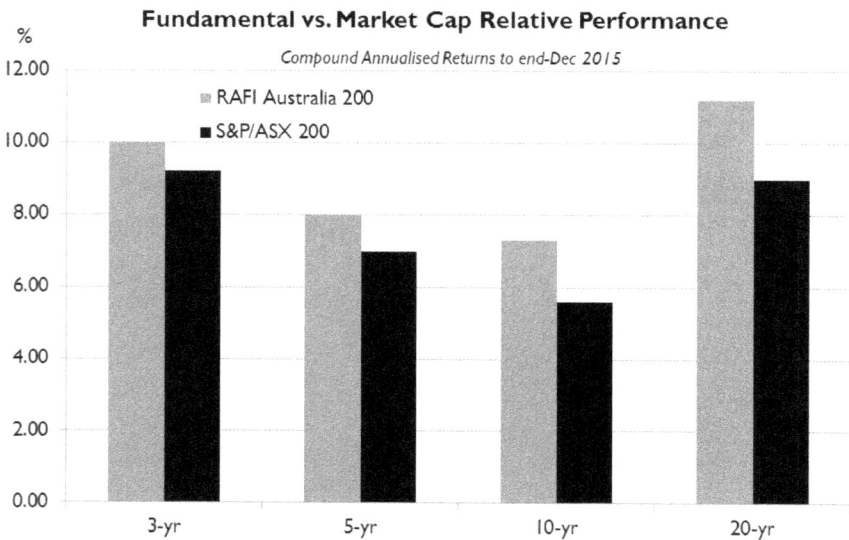

Fundamental vs. Market Cap Relative Performance

Compound Annualised Returns to end-Dec 2015

Legend: RAFI Australia 200; S&P/ASX 200

Period	RAFI Australia 200	S&P/ASX 200
3-yr	~10.0	~9.2
5-yr	~8.0	~6.9
10-yr	~7.2	~5.5
20-yr	~11.2	~9.0

This outperformance relative to a market-cap index makes intuitive sense, as it suggests stock prices tend to overshoot their underlying fundamentals on both the upside and downside over time. As seen in the diagram below, the attraction of a fundamentally-weighted index under these circumstances is that it effectively *overweights* stocks (compared with the market-cap index) when their prices seem relatively cheap compared with their underlying fundamentals (such as, earnings or book value), and *underweights* them when they are relatively expensive compared with fundamentals.

The fundamental index then benefits from "regression to the mean," whereby cheap stocks tend to enjoy price outperformance relative to their fundamentals and expensive stocks suffer price underperformance.

Fundamental vs. Market Cap Weighted Indices

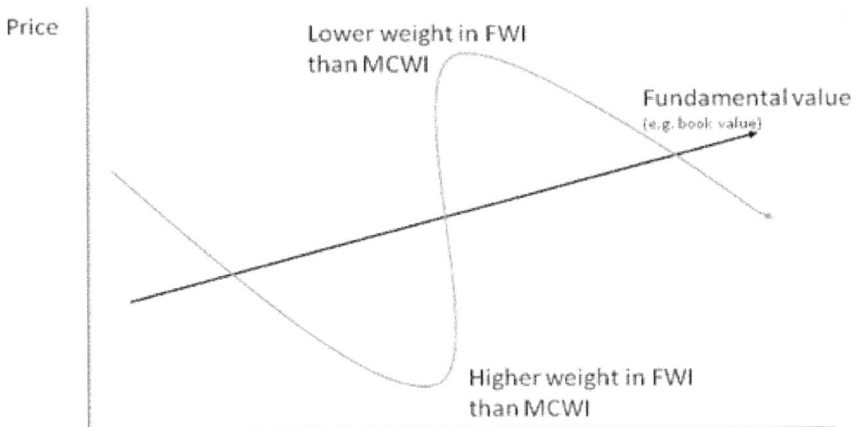

Of course, there will be times when a fundamentally weighted index may temporarily underperform a market cap index – when expensive stocks are still rallying on momentum (such as, tech stocks during the tech bubble), and when cheap stocks are still being sold down (such as, financials in the latter part of the global financial crisis).

Although past performance is never a guarantee of future performance, fundamentally weighted index methodologies appear to have a relatively good historic record – and the notion of a "regression to the mean" provides a reasonable theoretical underpinning for why they might tend to outperform traditional market-cap weighted indices over the long-term.

By contrast, the VanEck Vectors's MVW ETF tracks an "equal weighted" index, which invests in up to 76 of the largest (by market capitalisation) and most liquid stocks. It does, however, give each stock equal weight.

This means that companies, such as BHP-Billiton and the Commonwealth Bank, would typically have a weight of not more than 1.5%, compared with 8 to 10% in traditional market capitalisation weightings of the top 200 stocks. Effectively, this index places greater weight on smaller cap stocks and provides greater diversification across stocks than traditional market capitalisation indices. VanEck Vectors does not invest in more than 70 stocks, or so, as its research suggests not much added diversification (risk reduction) benefit is achieved beyond this level. The bias toward small caps in the index suggests this ETF will do relatively well when small caps are doing relatively well, as was the case in 2015. Over the 5-year period ending at the close of December 2015, the underlying index for the VanEck Vectors' MVW ETF generated an 8.6% annualised return – just above the 8% return for BetaShares' fundamentally-weighted index. Both indices, however, did outperform the S&P/ASX 200 Index's 7% return.

Proponents of both these alternate-weight indices argue they should be able to outperform the traditional market-cap weighted index over time. While they may lose out relative to market-cap indices in the short-term - when momentum in certain sectors and stocks is strong – this tends to be offset by outperformance once these "hot" areas correct back to fairer value.

The final ETP to note in this section is the UBS IQ MorningStar Australia Quality ETF.   This Fund tracks a rules-based equal-weight index that invests in approximately 25 to 50 Australian listed companies that MorningStar Research consider have "sustainable competitive advantages."   In the 3-years to June 2016, it achieved annualised returns of 8.5%, compared with 7.7% for the S&P/ASX 200 Index.

AUSTRALIAN SECTOR ETFS

Along with broad Australian equity market ETFs, there is also a growing range of equity sector based ETFs. However, these still primarily only cover the two dominant market sectors: financials (including listed property) and resources.   Many investment benchmarks are similar (or even identical), and therefore, should offer similar gross long-run investment performance.

Investors have a choice of investing in listed property, resources as a group (covering both the metal/mining and energy sectors), and/or financials, excluding listed property.

Listed property remains the most popular sector play, and State Street and Vanguard have the two most popular ETFs in this area.

Australian Equity Sector ETPs as at Dec 2015						
ASX Code	Product Type	Fund Name	ICR (%p.a.)*	FUM ($m)	# trades	Bid-Offer % spread
Listed Property						
MVA	ETF	VanEck Vectors Australian Property ETF	0.35	$46.8	80	0.19%
SLF	ETF	SPDR S&P/ASX 200 Listed Property Fund	0.40	$599.0	1,250	0.16%
VAP	ETF	Vanguard Australian Property Securities Index ETF	0.25	$521.0	1,640	0.23%
Resources						
MVE	ETF	VanEck Vectors Australian Emerging Resources ETF	0.49	$1.6	5	0.47%
MVR	ETF	VanEck Vectors Australian Resources ETF	0.35	$2.2	14	0.17%
OZR	ETF	SPDR S&P/ASX 200 Resource Fund	0.40	$20.9	101	0.31%
QRE	ETF	BetaShares S&P/ASX 200 Resources Sector ETF	0.39	$5.1	35	0.43%
Financials (ex-Listed Property)						
MVB	ETF	VanEck Vectors Australian Bank ETF	0.28	$24.4	220	0.10%
OZF	ETF	SPDR S&P/ASX 200 Financials ex A-REITs Fund	0.40	$60.0	406	0.10%
QFN	ETF	BetaShares S&P/ASX 200 Financials Sector ETF	0.39	$24.0	430	0.22%

It is worth noting that Vanguard now offers strong competition to State Street's long-established listed property ETF (SLF) covering the S&P/ASX 200 listed property sector ("or A-REITs") Sector.

Vanguard's ETF (VAP) covers the S&P/ASX 300 listed property sector - which produces virtually identical returns to the S&P/ASX 200 A-REITs index - but with an MER of only 0.25%, compared with a 0.40% MER for State Street's SLF. Covering 300, rather than 200, listed property stocks, Vanguard's ETF is also slightly more diversified. However, given the top heavy nature of the index, the differences in terms of company exposure and year-to-year investment performance are not great.

In both the S&P/ASX 200 and S&P/ASX 300 listed property sectors, for example, Westfield Group and the Westfield Retail Trust account for approximately 40% combined, while Stockland and Goodman Group account for roughly 10% each - meaning 60% of these indices are made up from only four companies.

Four major banks dominate the financial indices, accounting for around 70% of the financials (excluding listed property) benchmark. For investors that consider even this not enough banking exposure, VanEck Vectors offers a banking ETF (MVB) that is effectively the financial sector, excluding listed property and other non-banking financial firms (such as, asset management, custody, commercial lending, and insurance). This ETF does, however, include investment banks, such as Macquarie.

VanEck Vectors also provides some interesting variations in the resources space. Its Resources ETP (MVR) tracks a specially constructed resources index that includes both mining and mining-service companies (the latter typically being found in the industrials sector), and the weight per stock is capped at 8%. This means that large companies, such as BHP-Billiton, have no more than an 8% weight in the index, compared with a closer to 40% weight in the resource sector ETFs offered by State Street and BetaShares that track the traditional S&P/ASX 200 Resources index.

VanEck Vectors also offers a small-cap resource ETF that includes only those companies with a market capitalisation in the bottom 10% of the broader resources index.

Ethical ETFs

There are two ETFs on the Australian market that claim to accommodate the concerns of more "ethically minded" investors. The UBS ETF tracks the Australian MSCI index, but excludes "companies with significant business activities involving tobacco and those engaged in the production of cluster bombs, landmines, chemical and biological weapons, and depleted uranium weapons." This adjusted index comprises approximately 71 constituents listed on the Australian exchanges, and covers approximately 85% of the Australian free float-adjusted market capitalisation.

Australian Large Ethical ETPs as at Dec 2015						
ASX Code	Product Type	Fund Name	ICR (%p.a.)*	FUM ($m)	# trades	Bid-Offer % spread
UBA	ETF	UBS IQ MSCI Australian Ethical ETF	0.17	$77.9	8	0.14%
RARI	ETF	Russell Australian Responsible Investment ETF	0.45	$8.7	-	0.33%

The Russell ETF appears to be a little broader in terms of the companies it deems not sufficiently ethical or responsible. Like the UBS product, the Russell ETF excludes companies with exposure to tobacco and weaponry, but also excludes those with exposure to the manufacturing and/or distribution of alcohol, gambling, or pornography, as well as those involved in the production or combustion of more carbon-intensive fossil fuels. In addition, it may exclude companies that "lag industry peers in approaching [environmental, social, and governance] ESG risk."

So who's "unethical?" The UBS ETF includes gambling companies, such as Crown, Aristocrat, Tab Corp, and Woolworths, whereas the Russell ETF does not. Indeed, due to the very narrow definition of 'ethical' companies used by the UBS product, it's not clear whether the Australian index explicitly excludes any companies on ethical grounds alone. The Russell ETF, meanwhile, also excludes miners involved in greenhouse gas producing coal and petroleum production, such as BHP Billiton, Rio-Tinto, Santos and Woodside. These companies are all included in the UBS ETF.

Although both these ETFs were only recently launched, they are still likely to broadly track the performance of the broad large market cap indices described above. That said, the Russell ETF does appear to place less weight on mining stocks, which could affect relative performance when the mining sector is doing particular well or poorly relative to the broader market.

BEAR (OR SHORT) FUNDS

If you have a negative view of the overall Australian equity market, or are looking to protect your portfolio against a downturn, then the BetaShares "Australian Equities Bear Hedge Fund" (ASX code: BEAR) may be of interest. The Fund is designed to go up when the share market (as measured by the S&P/ASX 200 index) goes down, and vice versa.

Australian Equity Bear ETPs as at Dec 2015						
ASX Code	Product Type	Fund Name	ICR (%p.a.)*	FUM ($m)	# trades	Bid-Offer % spread
BEAR	MF	BetaShares Australian Equities Bear Hedge Fund	1.38	$58.0	739	0.13%
BBOZ	MF	BetaShares Australian Equties Strong Bear Hedge Fund	1.38	$33.0	2,004	0.14%

How? The Fund invests its investment proceeds in cash and then sells Australian equity index futures contracts (i.e. the ASX SPI 200 future), so that the Fund has an overall negative exposure to the market equal to around 100% of the Fund's value.

This Fund, therefore, enables investors to make money should the share market fall – as the futures contracts sold short can be bought back at lower prices, earning the Fund a trading profit. The Fund charges an annual management fee of 1.38%, and has approximately $58 million under management as of the end of December 2015.

The Fund does not use borrowing, or any other instrument (including derivatives), to leverage its returns (although market movements may cause the Fund to be slightly leveraged on any given day). All payment obligations relating to investments are met within the Fund, so that investors are not at risk of margin calls. Investors cannot lose more than their original investment. By using the Bear Hedge Fund, investors can avoid the complications and costs associated with more traditional ways of obtaining short market exposure, through CFDs, options, or futures.

This is an unleveraged fund, so if you want say $50,000 of negative exposure to the market, you need to buy $50,000 worth of the ASX-traded product. What's more, the Fund is flexibly managed so that its net short exposure can vary between 90% and 110% on any given day. This means that a 1% decline in the market on any given day should produce a rise in the Fund of between 0.9 to 1.1%, and vice-versa. This flexibility helps the Fund to avoid the need for strict daily re-balancing, which can lead to a performance drag over time in the face of day-to-day market changes. The actual exposure level on any given day appears on the BetaShares' website.

As seen in the chart below, the BEAR Fund has so far done a good job of moving in the opposite direction of the market without exhibiting major tracking errors or performance drag.

BetaShares BEAR Hedge Fund

Source:: Thomson Reuters

In the 12 months ending December 31, 2015, the BEAR Fund lost 2.4% in value while the S&P/ASX 200 accumulation index gained 2.6%. Since its inception in early July 2012, the Fund lost 8.9% at a time when the market rose 12.2%, so even over extended periods, the broad negative correlation has held true.

In April 2015, BetaShares launched the Australian Equities Strong Bear Hedge Fund (ASX Code: BBOZ). This is structured similarly to the Bear fund, however, the degree of negative exposure to the market is larger as it seeks to generate magnified returns that are negatively correlated with the returns of the Australian share market (as measured by the S&P/ASX 200 Index). On average, a 1% fall in the Australian share market on a given day can be expected to deliver a 2.0% to 2.75% increase in the value of the Strong Bear Hedge Fund (and vice versa), whereas it would only produce a 0.9% to 1.1% increase in the value of the Bear Hedge Fund.

As with Bear Fund above, the Strong Bear Fund does not require investors to explicitly take out loans or be subject to margin calls, as all borrowing is handled internally within the Fund.

As will be detailed in the international ETP section below, BetaShares also offers a similar bear/short strategy for the US S&P 500 index.

GEARED FUNDS

Also recently released onto the market is the BetaShares Geared Australian Equity Hedge Fund (ASX code: GEAR). The Fund aims to provide investors with a simple way to obtain a cost-effective geared exposure to Australian share market returns.

Australian Equity Geared ETPs as at Dec 2015						
ASX Code	Product Type	Fund Name	ICR (%p.a.)*	FUM ($m)	# trades	Bid-Offer % spread
GEAR	MF	BetaShares Geared Australian Equity Hedge Fund	0.80	$85.8	1,260	0.26%

How so? The fund combines proceeds from investors with borrowing to buy a broad portfolio of Australia's largest 200 listed stocks (as measured by the S&P/ASX 200 Index) – with a gearing ratio (total borrowing as a percent of total fund gross assets) of between 50-65%. At a 50% gearing, for example, it means the fund will borrow $100 for every $100 provided by investors, so as to invest $200 in the market.

At such a gearing level, the fund would have twice the exposure to market movements – if the market rises (falls) by 2%, the value of the fund's assets should rise (fall) by approximately 4 per cent. Of course, this also means the fund would earn twice the dividends (and franking credits) of an ungeared investment. However, it will also have to pay some interest costs on the borrowing involved, as well as the fund management fee.

As a per cent of the funds "gross asset value" (i.e., including both the investment capital and borrowed funds), the management fee is 0.8%. At a gearing ratio of 50%, however, this equates to a fee of 1.6% of investor funds, and 2.3% at a gearing ratio of 65%.

At face value, management fees may appear high. However, on closer inspection, compared with alternatives, such as margin loans, warrants, or unlisted geared funds, the total Fund cost is actually substantially lower. Indeed, compared with margin loans and warrants, the Fund has lower borrowing costs and is easier to invest in. While margin loans and warrants generally charge *retail* borrowing costs, the Fund can borrow on professional *wholesale* markets at considerably cheaper rates. And the Fund can be bought directly on the ASX, whereas margin loans and warrants require completion of often lengthy and complex loan agreement forms. If you have already signed up for a share broking account, you have already signed all the forms you need to buy into the Fund.

Unlike warrants, moreover, the Fund is not subject to the same "counterparty" risk that a warrant issuer might get into financial difficulty, which risks investor capital.

Unlike traditional margin loans, moreover, there are no margin calls for investors – as all borrowing is undertaken by the Fund, not individual investors. If the market falls, (raising gearing levels) assets are sold to reduce investor exposure. This does mean that in extreme cases, however, investors could still face a significant capital loss.

That said, the same is true for geared investments through warrants and margin loans, whereas the latter also leaves investors at risk of losing more than their initial invested capital. Another positive is that, as with many Australian equity funds, the Fund is structured to provide investors with both dividends *and* franking tax credits, due to the fact that the corporate income tax has already been paid before dividends are distributed.

What's more, due to low borrowing costs and leverage, dividend proceeds usually more than fully offset the borrowing cost, meaning the Fund does not require investors to make regular contributions to pay interest costs. In fact, the Fund should still be able to make net distributions (after borrowing costs) to investors over time.

For example, with 50% gearing, interest costs assumed at 3.5%, and a 4% assumed market dividend yield, a $100 investment in the Fund would return $8 in dividends (even after a management fee assumed at 0.8%). As outlined in the table below, the effective after-tax return on this dividend would be $4.43, or 4.4%. By contrast, an un-geared $100 investment – even with a lower management fee assumed at 0.29% – would generate an after-tax return of only $3.80, or 3.8%.

Geared vs. Non-Geared Funds				
	Investor Equity	$	100	100
	Gearing ratio		50%	0%
	Total Investment	$	200	100
	Dividend Yield		4.0%	4.0%
a	Dividend	$	8.0 $	4.0
b	Grossed-Up	$	11.4 $	5.7
	Interest rate (%)		3.5%	0.0%
c	Interest cost ($)	$	3.5 $	-
	Management fee (%)		0.8%	0.29%
d	Management fee ($)	$	1.6 $	0.3
	Net taxable income[1]	$	6.33 $	5.42
	Gross Tax payable (30%)	$	1.9 $	1.6
e	*less franking credit* [2]	$	3.43 $	1.71
f	Net tax payable	-$	1.5 -$	0.09
	After-tax cash return[3]	$	4.43 $	3.80
	Return on investment		4.4%	3.8%

1. b-c-d

2. b/(1-30%)-b

3. a-c-d-f

As with a warrant, but unlike the typical margin loan, it is possible to invest in the Fund – gaining leveraged exposure to the market – through a SMSF.

One issue with the Fund, as structured, is possible performance drag due to the need to adjust gearing levels in the face of market volatility. Note that if the market rises, the Fund's gearing ratio will fall, possibly requiring the Fund to eventually borrow more and buy more equities, so as to keep the gearing ratio within the permitted range. By contrast, if the market falls, the gearing ratio will rise, possibly requiring the Fund to sell equities to reduce gearing back to the permitted range. As a result, a performance drag could be created over time to the extent the market is volatile, since the Fund will need to buy more stock when prices are relatively high, and sell when prices are relatively low.

That said, the Fund is structured to reduce this potential performance drag, by allowing the gearing ratio to vary within a band. This reduces the need for regular rebalancing – on a daily or even weekly basis – to maintain gearing levels in the face of modest market volatility, which in turn reduces the risk of continually "buying high and selling low."

Another issue to bear in mind is that unlike some other geared investment products – like margin loans and listed warrants – it is not possible for investors in the Fund to pre-pay interest costs just before the end of the financial year to get an upfront tax deduction.

As will be detailed in the international ETP section below, BetaShares also offers a similar geared strategy covering the US S&P 500 index.

MANAGED RISK ETPS

Hot off the presses at the time of this writing, another variant to the traditional broad equity ETF, the BetaShares Managed Risk Australian Share Fund was introduced (ASX Code: AUST).

Australian Managed Risk Equity ETPs as at Dec 2015						
ASX Code	Product Type	Fund Name	ICR (%p.a.)*	FUM ($m)	# trades	Bid-Offer % spread
AUST	MF	BetaShares Managed Risk Australian Share Fund (Managed Fund)	0.49	$6.0	19	0.23%

AUST offers core exposure to the top 200 Australia stocks weighted by market capitalisation, allowing investors the benefit of capital growth, dividends, and franking credits associated with owning these stocks within the Fund. However, on top of this, the Fund also actively monitors share market volatility and, when volatility rises, applies a "handbrake" to reduce the impact of major market declines. This reduced risk exposure is achieved by selling equity index futures contracts (i.e. ASX SPI 200 futures), so that the Fund is effectively hedged against market declines (to a certain degree).

Exactly how much the Fund is hedged on any given day will depend on market conditions. The Fund employs quantitative rules run in conjunction with Milliman, one of the world's largest institutional risk managers. Milliman's risk management strategies have been used for the last 15 years by some of the largest firms and institutional investors in the world and have previously helped institutional clients (i.e., other fund managers) navigate both the 'tech bubble' and the global financial crisis.

The Fund's aim is to provide investors with an alternative means of reducing downside portfolio risk – which is especially important for those near to or in retirement – without having to simply increase exposure to low yield cash or fixed income products. Instead, the Fund aims to expose investors to the majority (but not all) of the upside potential of the Australian share market, with the benefit of potentially avoiding the majority (but not all) of the downside of declining markets.

As will be detailed in the international ETP section below, BetaShares also offers a similar managed risk strategy over the MSCI (Developed Market) World Equity Index.

HIGH YIELD ETPS

Given growing demand for higher and steadier income returns from those approaching or in retirement, a suite of "high income" ETPs are now also available on the Australian market. These have quickly proven to be extremely popular.

Using their own proprietary stock selection methodology, these ETPs attach a higher weight to stocks with relatively large and steady dividends. Most ETP providers generally aim to match the broader market's price returns over time, though simultaneously achieve a higher and steadier than average dividend yield.

This compares with the typical market capitalisation weighted ETF – such as State Street's S&P/ASX 200 SPDR Fund (STW) - that attaches the highest weight to stocks with the highest market capitalisation. All four of Australia's major exchange traded fund managers, iShares, State Street, Vanguard, and BetaShares, have launched their own version of a high-income ETP. Most other ETP providers have also launched funds of their own. It's fair to say the high yield space has become a fairly crowded market!

ASX Code	Product Type	Fund Name	ICR (%p.a.)*	FUM ($m)	# trades	Bid-Offer % spread
AOD	MF	Aurora Dividend Income Trust	1.27	$15.6	32	1.18%
DIV	ETF	UBS IQ MorningStar Australian Dividend Yield ETF	0.30	$23.3	14	0.24%
HVST	MF	BetaShares Australian Dividend Harvester Fund (managed fund)	0.90	$136.7	353	0.17%
IHD	ETF	iShares S&P/ASX High Dividend Yield	0.30	$239.3	484	0.28%
RDV	ETF	Russell High Dividend Australian Shares ETF	0.34	$278.6	382	0.29%
SYI	ETF	SPDR MSCI Australia Select High Dividend Yield Fund	0.35	$150.0	197	0.11%
VHY	ETF	Vanguard Australian Shares High Yield ETF	0.25	$629.3	1,726	0.16%
YMAX	MF	BetaShares Australian Top 20 Equity Yield Maximiser Fund (managed fund)	0.79	$345.6	1,824	0.19%
ZYAU	ETF	ANZ ETFS S&P/ASX 300 High Yield Plus ETF	0.35	$3.0	29	0.31%
FDIV**	ETF	VanEck Vectors S&P/ASX Franked Dividend ETF	0.35	-	-	-

Australian Equity Dividend/Income ETPs as at Dec 2015

**FDIV launched in April 2016

As is typical from Vanguard, its product (ASX Code: VHY) offers the cheapest high yield ETP with a management expense ratio of only 0.25%. It is now also the largest high-yield ETP, with funds under management of $629m, as of the end of 2015. BetaShares' Equity Yield Maximiser Fund (ASX: YMAX) is in second place, with $345m funds under management.

With the exception of Aurora's AOD, all ETPs appear to have similar degrees of liquidity, as measured by the average bid-offer spreads in December 2015.

It should be noted that by chasing yield, these ETPs often end up with sector exposures different from the overall market – typically more concentrated in financials and consumer staples, and less in materials/resources. But, each provider also differs in the risk limits placed on each sector. These sector differences should be considered in light of the other sector exposures in your portfolio.

The table below (which does not allow for franking credits) indicates the extent of enhanced yield return that is possible though overweighting stocks and sectors with above-average dividend yields[12]. According to ASX data, the historic distribution yield for most high dividend ETPs ranged from 6 to 10% over 2015, compared with yields of around 4% for market-cap weighted ETPS, such as STW and VAS.

While on the subject of income returns, note that the "distribution yield" often quoted for an ETP product is not always equal to its "dividend" or "income" yield. That's because distributions sometimes include capital gains as when a fund is required to sell an underlying security such as when a large company leaves the index that the ETP tracks.

In 2015, for example, 21st Century Fox (which had split from New Corp) was removed from major Australian equity indices, which required some ETPs holding the stock to sell it. This, in turn, involved some capital being returned to investors. Distributions can also be boosted in a given year due to capital returns by companies, as undertaken by Qantas in 2015.

---

[12] ZYAU was excluded as it has not had a full year of distributions.

Historical Distribution Yield*

%

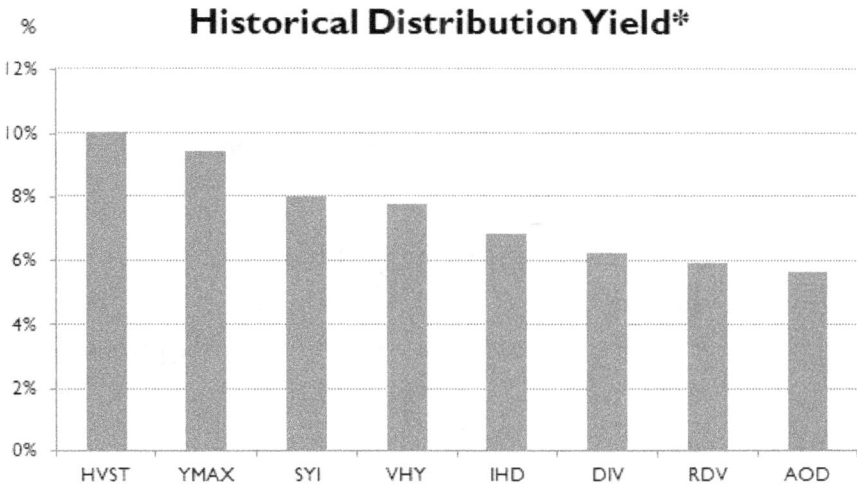

*Source: ASX Monthly Funds Update. Yield is for 12 months to end-December 2015

As we'll now see, moreover, there are other ways to generate enhanced yield apart from simply investing in stocks that offer high dividends.

BetaShares' Covered Call Strategy

BetaShares' ETP, YMAX, for example, aims to provide attractive income through implementing a "covered call" or "buy write" options strategy. This involves earning option premiums (and hence income for investors in the Fund) by selling (or "writing") exchange-traded call options on up to 100% of the securities in the share portfolio. This strategy also effectively provides a partial hedge against a decline in the value of the share portfolio, as some of the capital lost from a decline in share prices is offset by the earned option premium.

By selling call options (with calls being the right to buy shares at some point in the future at a pre-determined price), over the shares you own, you are effectively agreeing to forgo some upside capital gain potential on these shares (should share prices rise strongly), in exchange for the options premium income. For example, imagine a share is trading at $9 and you sell a call option for 50c, giving someone else the right (but, not the obligation) to buy your shares for $10[13] at the end of 3-months.

If the share's price rises to $15 – the call holder will exercise their option and stand to make a net $4.50 profit (the capital gain from reselling the share less the cost of the option). If share prices stay at or below $10, however, you don't need to sell your shares. Either way, you still get to keep your 50c call premium income. But, even if the share's price is above $10, you at least make $1 capital gain on the sale (from the current $9 price), plus the option income – or $1.50.

Accordingly, in a share market which is trending sideways or falling, the buy/write strategy is likely to add value compared to the share portfolio alone as relatively little, if any, share portfolio capital gain is forgone in exchange for the earned option premiums. Returns should be further enhanced by the tendency of option premiums to increase during periods of market turbulence.

During periods when the market rises more strongly, however, the buy/write strategy may detract from performance, as relatively more capital gain is forgone. But, even in these latter periods, the buy/write strategy should still help to dampen return volatility relative to the share portfolio without the buy/write strategy, through the option premiums received.

---

[13] The price at which call buyers are able to buy the stock under such agreements is known as the "strike" price.

BetaShares actively manages the call options exposures, which are typically written with expiry terms of one to three months, and at strike prices that are expected to be approximately 3% to 7% above the then current market prices for the shares in question, subject to prevailing volatility.

According to research by the Australian Securities Exchange[14], buy-write strategies, similar to those used by BetaShares, were able to provide enhanced risk-adjusted returns – compared to a long-only portfolio – over the period from April 2005 to December 2011. This, admittedly, was an overall sluggish period for stocks – with outperformance most evident during the extended period of flat or falling share prices, partly offset by underperformance during a shorter bull market period. As will be detailed in the international ETP section below, BetaShares also offers a similar strategy over the US S&P 500 index.

BetaShares Dividend Harvester Fund

Another innovative strategy offered by BetaShares is embedded in the Australian Dividend Harvester Fund (ASX Code: HVST). The Fund aims to provide investors with exposure to large capitalisation Australian shares, along with regular franked dividend income, paid monthly, that is at least double the annual income yield of the broad Australian share market. In addition, the Fund also offers a "risk management" strategy identical to that of the Managed Risk Australian Equity Fund (AUST) described above.

---

[14] Source: ASX Market Insights, *"An Encyclopaedia of Australian Buy-Write Returns"* (August 2012).

Unlike AUST – which retains core exposure in the market's top 200 stocks – HVST uses a dividend "harvesting" strategy to gain exposure to 14 or more Australian securities (from among the top 50 market capitalisation stocks) that are expected within approximately the next two months to provide the highest gross yield outcomes (based on declared dividends or analyst consensus). After this period, the Fund is rebalanced with a new selection of stocks expected to provide the highest gross yield outcomes for the following two months. For any given rebalancing period, if there is not a sufficient number of stocks that meet the yield threshold, then one or more ASX exchange traded funds with broad Australian share market exposure will be added to the portfolio, increasing Fund diversification.

Utilising this strategy, investors gain some exposure to the underlying capital growth of the securities held over the relevant two month period, but more importantly, a source of relatively high regular dividend income potential, in addition to the benefit of any associated franking credits.

At the same time, the Fund's risk management strategy involves fully or partially hedging overall market exposure – by selling ASX SPI 200 futures – as is the case with AUST.

That said, one extra source of potential volatility in the case of HVST (unlike for AUST) is the *stock specific risk* associated with holding around 14 individual stocks at any given time. If, as happened in early 2015, the market sees fit to sell down bank stocks at a time when HVST is holding several of them, there is the occasional risk of underperformance relative to the market - even with the broader risk market management strategy still in place.

Due to the risk management strategy being in place and the larger relatively stable income component, moreover, the overall volatility of HVST *total returns* may well be somewhat less than for the overall market, notwithstanding the stock specific risk mentioned above.

Another issue to bear in mind is that, unless at least some of the income generated from HVST's strategy is reinvested, investors may be exposed to some degree of capital erosion over time (i.e., the unit price will tend to decline somewhat over time), even though the *total return* from holding the Fund (i.e., income plus capital) may be similar (or even better) over the long-run to that of the market as a whole.

After all, the nature of HVST's stock rotation strategy means it will likely be buying stocks in which an element of the dividend about to be paid is already reflected in their price. This will then be priced out as dividends are paid out.

For example, if the total return of both the market and HVST were 10% p.a., and HVST produced a 12% income return, then in a purely efficient market, HVST's capital value would decline 2% p.a.

Of course, if desired, the extent of any capital erosion could be easily ameliorated through a partial reinvestment of some of the Fund's income proceeds. Indeed, the Fund provides the option of reinvesting all or any part of income distributions through HVST's Dividend Reinvestment Plan.

What's more, countering this potential capital erosion effect is some evidence[15] that markets are not fully efficient. Stock prices do not always fully adjust downwards to reflect the value of dividends paid out.

One potential reason for this is that fund managers tend to prefer capital gains over income returns (as handling the latter distributions can be administratively cumbersome). They also don't fully value the benefit of franking credits, as they're not assessed by their "grossed up" performance.

As a result, fund managers may be sellers during the pre-dividend payment period as prices are being run-up, and buyers once stocks have gone ex-dividend – a process which may lessen the degree to which shares prices fully adjust to reflect the value of dividends (including franking credits) paid.

To the extent that stock prices don't fully adjust over time as dividends are paid, it will lessen the degree of capital erosion.

Aurora Dividend Income Trust

Another high income-oriented strategy is provided by the Aurora Dividend Income Trust (ASX Code: AOD) by Aurora Funds Limited. This fund predominantly invests in a portfolio of fully franked dividend paying companies listed on the ASX, while employing a "risk management overlay" to limit exposure to Australian equities to around 50% of net assets. It does this by short-selling non-fully franked dividend paying companies (equal to around 50% of the Fund's value), taking the view that fully

[15] *The Ex-Dividend Performance of ASX200 Stocks Measured Against the 45-Day Holding Rule (January 2000 – March 2011)* ASX Market Insights June 2011.

franked dividend paying companies should outperform non-fully franked dividend paying companies over the long-run.

Aurora aims to make cash distributions of at least 1.5% per quarter and distribute more franking credits each year than could be achieved by an equivalent investment in the S&P/ASX 200 index.

Aurora argues the Fund should outperform during market downturns, but underperform during upturns. However, the overall aim is to outperform the broader market over a rolling 5-year period, based on the expectation that fully franked dividend paying companies will tend to outperform the broader market.

Aurora's strategy to always distribute at least 1.5% of net assets as cash, plus any available franking credits per quarter - regardless of performance - means that if there is insufficient net income in a given quarter, investors may receive a partial (or full) return of capital, with associated capital gains tax consequences.

OTHER "STRATEGIC" OR ACTIVELY MANAGED FUNDS

At the time of writing, there was one other Australian equity ETFs that use certain criteria to pick stocks other than simply market capitalisation, sector exposure, or dividend yield.

Russell's "Australian Value" (ASX Code RVL) was launched in May 2011 and selects a sub-set of Australian large cap stocks (typically around 40 to 60 stocks) that, in the words of Russell, "demonstrate value characteristics," as determined by their price to earnings (PE) ratio and consensus-based medium-term earnings expectations. Russell chooses 40 to 60 large cap stocks on the market that appear to have a relatively low price-to-current earnings ratios given their expected earnings growth profile. As a result, they could be considered relatively good "value."

Australian Other Strategic ETPs as at Dec 2015						
ASX Code	Product Type	Fund Name	ICR (%p.a.)*	FUM ($m)	# trades	Bid-Offer % spread
RVL	ETF	Russell Australian Value ETF	0.34	$22.9	31	0.30%

As noted in the small cap section above, K2 Asset Management's small cap fund (ASX Code: KSM) is also actively managed, and aims to beat traditional small cap benchmarks over time.

Another notable entrant into the actively managed space is the Magellan Financial Group, which will be detailed in the international equity ETF section below. In April 2016, BetaShares also announced a strategic alliance with AMP Capital to jointly launch a series of active exchange traded managed funds.

INTERNATIONAL EQUITY ETPS

As of end of 2015, there were 51 international equity ETPs on the local market – providing exposure to a range of markets, including: the United States, Europe, Japan, and China. There are also more broadly diversified regional ETFs that provide exposure to developed and/or emerging markets, or global industries, such as health care, consumer staples, and telecommunications. Investors also have a choice between hedged and non-currency hedged funds; those with an ethical or value focus, and even three actively managed exchange traded funds.

A WORD ON CURRENCY HEDGING

Currency "hedging" effectively means that investors' offshore returns are protected from foreign currency declines against the $A ($A appreciation). However, by the same token, they miss out on added returns when foreign currencies appreciate against the $A. During the commodity boom between 2003 and 2011, for example, investors' returns from offshore markets were dented by strong gains in the $A – as any foreign returns were worth less when later converted back into $A's. By contrast, the sharp decline in the $A since mid-2011 has boosted international returns.

Whether to hedge or not is really up to the investor. By hedging, investors are able to simplify their investment process by being able to make a purer "bet" on the relative performance of the Australian vs. international equity markets (based on, say, relative valuations, relative economic performance, or sector exposures).

That said, if investors have a strong view that the $A will rise (such as, for example, when the $A is very expensive relative to its long-run average), then hedging might be a reasonable option to enhance offshore returns.

Over the very long-run, the choice between hedging or not should not make much difference if the $A remains relatively stable, which is possible if local inflation does vary significantly with global trends.

Note, moreover, returns from the hedged ETPs will also be affected by the relative interest costs of maintaining hedges over time. For example, if Australian interest rates are generally higher than those globally, then a currency hedged ETP will produce an added *positive* interest rate return, since investors are effectively borrowing (shorting) foreign currencies at cheaper rates to buy exposure to the $A that offers a higher interest rate return.

However, if local interest rates fall below those internationally, such a hedge will detract from ETP returns, since it involves borrowing currencies at higher interest rates to invest in $A's which offer a lower interest rate return.

GLOBAL VS. AUSTRALIAN PERFORMANCE

As seen in the chart below, after a long period of underperformance versus Australian shares during the Chinese-led commodity boom and global financial crisis, international equities have tended to outperform since late 2009, and especially since the commodity price peak in mid-2011.

World vs. Australian Equity Performance

Index Dec'95 = 100   MSCI All Country Index vs S&P/ASX 200

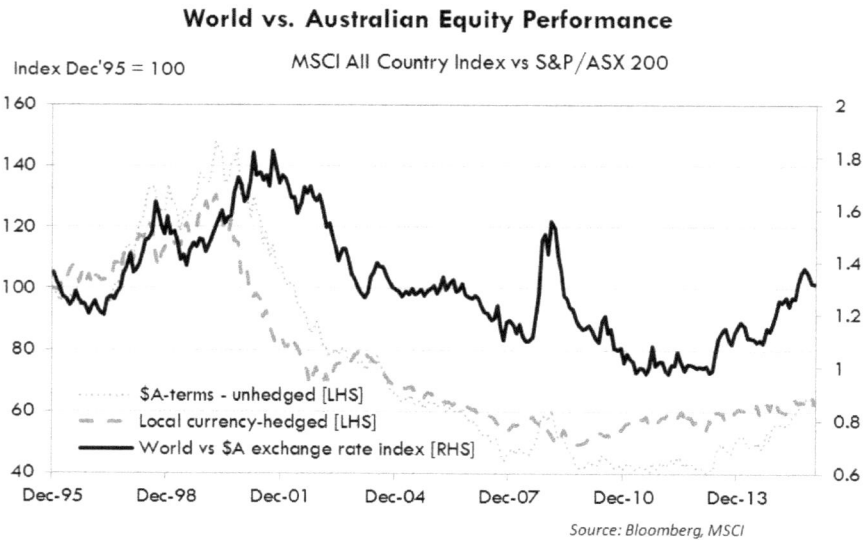

$A-terms - unhedged [LHS]
Local currency-hedged [LHS]
World vs $A exchange rate index [RHS]

Source: Bloomberg, MSCI

In currency unhedged terms, however, some of this early outperformance was offset by the continued strength in the Australian dollar. But, with the fall in the $A since 2011, international equity outperformance has been even greater in unhedged versus hedged terms

These swings in relative performance highlight the benefits of diversifying one's portfolio to include both Australian and international shares. After all, Australia still accounts for not much more than 2% of global stock market capitalisation. Our market is also top-heavy with resource and financial stocks, and especially underweight on technology stocks which have displayed good global outperformance as of late.

If the $A falls further in coming years, due to commodity price weaknesses, it will tend to assist unhedged currency exposure to foreign equity markets. Foreign markets will also outperform – irrespective of currency effects – if sectors relatively more important to the global economy than Australia (such as, technology or consumer stocks) outperform again, as last seen in the late 1990s. Relatively poor performance by mining stocks – which may occur if China's economic growth slows abruptly - would also tend to lead to the Australian market underperforming the global market.

BROAD (DEVELOPED COUNTRY) INTERNATIONAL ETPS

As seen in the table below, there are many broad international equity ETPs in Australia. These generally focus on developed markets, with emerging markets normally treated separately.

For example, the most common benchmark against which actively managed locally based international equity funds assess their performance is the MSCI (Developed Markets) World Index, excluding Australia. This index is tracked by both State Street's ETF (ASX Code:WXOZ) and Vanguards's (ASX Code:VGS).

This index assigns a large weight of around 55-60% to the United States, and just under 10% to Japan, while the remaining 30% or so is allocated to Europe. The top stocks in this index include: Apple (2%), Microsoft (1%), and Exxon Mobil (1%), along with Novartis, Johnson & Johnson, and General Electric to a lesser degree. The index is highly diversified, with the top ten stocks accounting for only around 10% of the overall index. By contrast, the top ten stocks in Australia account for around 50% of the S&P/ASX 200 index.

Both State Street and Vanguard also offer a hedged version of this broad international ETF – meaning investors can choose whether they want to hedge their currency exposure or not. If you feel the $A has a lot further to fall in coming years, then an unhedged exposure might be the better bet (this will naturally depend on your currency view).

Broad International Equity ETPs as at Dec 2015*						
ASX Code	Product Type	Fund Name	ICR (%p.a.)*	FUM ($m)	# trades	Bid-Offer % spread
Broad based						
IOO	ETF	iShares S&P Global 100	0.40	$1,062.7	2,011	0.17%
IHOO	ETF	iShares Global 100 AUD Hedged	0.46	$74.9	170	0.45%
WXOZ	ETF	SPDR S&P World ex Australian Fund	0.30	$141.6	127	0.22%
WXHG	ETF	SPDR S&P World ex Australian (Hedged) Fund	0.35	$70.0	402	0.27%
VGAD	ETF	Vanguard MSCI Index International Shares (Hedged) ETF	0.21	$61.7	879	0.23%
VGS	ETF	Vanguard MSCI-ex Australia Index International Shares ETF	0.18	$180.1	1,150	0.18%
IWLD	ETF	iShares MSCI World All Cap	0.16	-	-	-
IHWL	ETF	iShares MSCI World All Cap - Currency Hedged	0.19	-	-	-
Alternate Weights						
UBW	ETF	UBS IQ MSCI World ex Australia Ethical ETF	0.35	$10.4	52	0.28%
QUAL	ETF	Market Vectors MSCI World Ex-Australia Quality ETF	0.75	$80.8	413	0.28%
QMIX	ETF	SPDR MSCI World Quality Mix Fund	0.40	$3.1	17	0.36%
Income Focus						
WDIV	ETF	SPDR S&P Global Dividend Fund	0.50	$73.2	380	0.29%
Actively Managed						
KII	MF	K2 Global Equities Fund (Hedge Fund)	2.05	$45.9	119	0.73%
MGE	MF	Magellan Global Equities Fund (Managed Fund)	1.35	$436.5	2,198	0.39%
MHG	MF	Magellan Global Equities Fund Currency Hedged (Managed Fund)	1.35	$19.2	46	n/a
Managed Risk						
WRLD	MF	BetaShares Managed Risk Global Share Fund (Managed Fund)	0.54	$2.0	2	n/a

*IWLD & IHWL since April 2016

iShares also offers a broad global ETF (ASX Code: IOO), which has similar country exposures to the MSCI index above, though it only tracks the largest 100 global companies by market capitalisation. Since it has been around the longest, IOO retains the most funds under management in this category. iShares also offers a currency hedged version.

iShares in mid-2016 also launched hedged and unhedged ETFs that track the MSCI Developed Markets Index, *including* Australia. These ETFs are competitively priced, with the unhedged version now the cheapest (at 0.16%) in this broad global equity space, followed by Vanguard's VGS at 0.18%.   Note the difference between the MSCI Indices including and excluding Australia is quite marginal, given we account for only around 2.5% of the global index.

Alternative weights

There are variants in the broad global equity area. VanEck Vectors, for example, offers an ETF (ASX Code: QUAL) that tracks the MSCI World ex-Australia "quality' index. A quality company is one that the MSCI scores highly with respect to three key fundamental factors: high return on equity; stable year-on-year earnings growth; and low financial leverage. In a sense, it's the type of qualities that Warren Buffett likes to see when investing in companies. Whether this works in aggregate across all global markets remains to be seen – though VanEck Vectors cites MSCI research indicating its "quality" index has outperformed the more traditional market-cap weighted MSCI World index over the past two decades.

For those who are ethically minded, UBS also provides an index which excludes companies with "significant business activities involving tobacco and those engaged in the production of cluster bombs, landmines, chemical and biological weapons, and depleted uranium weapons." At the time of writing, the top 10 stocks in the UBS index were the same as those in the broader MSCI World ex-Australia Index, as tracked by Vanguard and State Street's ETFs. While the difference in return performance against other "less ethical" indices is likely to be marginal - given the small differences in constituent weights - it might nonetheless particularly interest conscientious investors who want to sleep more comfortably at night.

Income Focused

There is one broad global ETP with a specific income focus, WDIV from State Street. Unlike most of the instruments described above, this ETF *does* also cover emerging markets to a limited degree (with China and Brazil currently having a small weight of 1% each), though the main focus of the index it tracks is to include high dividend-yield companies "that have followed a managed-dividends policy of increasing or stable dividends for at least ten consecutive years." This ETF, therefore, aims to provide broad unhedged exposure to global stocks and generate a higher than average dividend yield than that of ETFs that track purely market-cap weighted indices. As of the end of 2015, the estimated dividend yield for this ETF was 5.3%, compared with only 2.7% for State Street's purely market-cap weighted variant, WXOZ.

Actively Managed

Rather than track a specific index, there are also three actively managed ETPs offered by Magellan and K2 Asset Management.

Both groups have effectively created an ETP version of their longer-standing unlisted flagship funds. The longer established (unlisted) Magellan Global Equities Fund boasts a 5-yr annualised return of 19.8% (net of fees), compared with 13.3% for the MSCI World Equity Index. Given such strong performance (the Fund has, so far at least, clearly been an outlier in terms of an active fund's ability to outperform a passive index) it's no surprise its unlisted fund has attracted a lot of funds under management, and its recently launched ETP version has already amassed $436m FUM as of the end of 2015. Magellan also offer a currency hedged version of the same fund.

The K2 unlisted fund can also point to reasonable performance, with a 5-year annualised return of 14.7% (net of fees).

What's also interesting with regard to both Magellan and K2's funds is that, as exchange traded products, they are able to be bought and sold on the ASX through the trading day at prices reasonably close to each fund's NAV due to active intra-day market making. This therefore avoids the problem of price discounts or premiums to NAV associated with listed investment companies. To protect each Fund's proprietary information, they only release specific stock holdings on a quarterly basis with a two month lag.

Managed Risk

As with AUST above, BetaShares also offers a global managed-risk ETP covering global equities, WRLD. The Fund provides exposure to global shares (generally consisting of at least 1,500 of the largest companies listed on the stock exchanges of the world's major developed economies, weighted by market capitalisation).

It also actively monitors share market volatility and, when volatility rises, applies a "handbrake" to reduce the impact of major market declines. This reduced risk exposure is achieved by selling equity index futures contracts that cover major global equity markets in Europe, Asia, and the United States.

WORLD EX-USA

There are currently two ETFs that focus on global stocks, excluding those of the United States. Vanguard's VEU covers the MSCI All-World Index ex-USA, meaning it also covers emerging markets – which have an approximately 18% share. iShares EAFE ETF (ASX Code: IVE) excludes both emerging markets and the United States, meaning it attaches a higher weight to Japan (22%), the United Kingdom (19%), and much of its remaining exposure is distributed across Europe.

International EquityWorld-ex USA ETPs as at Dec 2015						
ASX Code	Product Type	Fund Name	ICR (%p.a.)*	FUM ($m)	# trades	Bid-Offer % spread
VEU	ETF	Vanguard All-World ex US Shares Index ETF	0.14	$596.8	2,139	0.19%
IVE	ETF	iShares MSCI EAFE	0.33	$271.7	511	0.26%

UNITED STATES

The United States equity market is the most important and widely watched market in the world.   Investors that want some international exposure, but also want to focus on the United States (say because they know and follow that market the most), also have a range of US equity ETPs to choose from.

A US ETP can also be combined with an ETP that tracks all global markets, excluding the US (such as Vanguard's VEU), to obtain a very diversified global portfolio.

S&P 500 Index

As seen in the table below, ETPs that track the well-known S&P 500 index are most common – with the oldest and most popular (in terms of FUM) being iShare's IVV. As this is a cross-listing of a much larger US-based fund, scale economies allow the management fee on this ETP to be only 0.07% (no the decimal point is not in the wrong place!). iShares also offers a hedged version of this fund, with a modestly higher MER to cover the extra administrative expense. State Street has also recently launched its own S&P 500 fund.   In addition, iShares also offers separate exposure to the S&P mid-cap and small-cap indices.

US Equity Based ETPs as at Dec 2015						
ASX Code	Product Type	Fund Name	ICR (%p.a.)*	FUM ($m)	# trades	Bid-Offer % spread
S&P Market Cap						
IVV	ETF	iShares Core S&P 500	0.07	$2,006.6	2,392	0.06%
IHVV	ETF	iShares S&P 500 AID Hedged	0.13	$30.5	81	0.33%
SPY	ETF	SPDR S&P 500 ETF Trust	0.09	$21.6	39	0.37%
IJH	ETF	iShares Core S&P Midcap	0.12	$81.5	131	0.33%
IJR	ETF	iShares Core S&P Small-Cap	0.12	$46.2	105	0.39%
S&P Income Focused						
UMAX	MF	BetaShares S&P 500 Yield Maximser Fund (Managed Fund)	0.79	$58.7	352	0.21%
ZYUS	ETF	ANZ ETFS S&P 500 High Yield Low Volatility ETF	0.35	$7.3	50	0.33%
Other US Indices						
IRU	ETF	iShares Russell 2000	0.20	$53.4	164	0.32%
NDQ	ETF	BetaShares NASDAQ 100 ETF	0.48	$49.9	375	0.23%
MOAT	ETF	VanEck Vectors Morningstar Wide Moat ETF	0.49	$2.6	24	0.32%
QUS	ETF	BetaShares FTSE RAFI US 1000 ETF	0.40	$11.1	27	0.23%
UBU	ETF	UBS IQ MSCI USA Ethical ETF	0.20	$2.6	8	0.25%
VTS	ETF	Vanguard US Total Market Shares Index ETF	0.05	$824.2	1,843	0.10%
Bear and Gear Funds						
BBUS	MF	BetaShares US Equities Strong Bear Hedge Fund -Currency Hedged	1.38	$12.5	189	0.29%
GGUS	MF	BetaShares Geared US Equity Fund - Currency Hedged (Hedge Fund)	0.80	$6.5	50	0.43%

Income Focused

Two variants on simply tracking the market-cap weighted S&P 500 index come from BetaShares and the ANZ Bank, which provide a specific income focus.

Similar to BetaShares' YMAX ETP described in the Australian equity section above, BetaShares' UMAX invests in stocks comprising the S&P 500 Index but overlays this with a "buy-write" options strategy to boost income returns from the sale of call options. Unlike YMAX – where options are sold against individual stocks held by the Fund – UMAX simply sells call options against the S&P 500 index itself.

To get an idea of the extra income premium possible, over 2015, the historic distribution yield for UMAX (according to ASX estimates) was 6.1%, compared with only 1.8% for iShare's IVV (which tracks the S&P 500 without an options overlay). That said, YMAX did produce a somewhat lower capital return than IVV in 2015 as, due to the nature of its options strategy, it did not participate in all of the market's reasonably good 8.4% gain for the year. Overall, however, YMAX still managed to produce a total return 1% higher than that of IVV. More generally, UMAX's strategy has the potential to outperform the US stock market in most periods other than when stock prices are rising relatively strongly.

Another recent entrant in the US S&P 500 space is ANZ's S&P 500 "High Yield Low Volatility" ETF. This ETF first selects the top 75 dividend yielding stocks in the S&P 500 index and then picks 50 of those stocks with the lowest returns' volatility. Compared to the broader S&P 500 Index, this Index tends to be overweight on utilities, telecommunications, financials, and industrials, while being underweight on health care and technology.

Other US Equity Indices

There is a range of other US ETFs to choose from:

The iShares Russell 2000 index is much broader in scope than the S&P 500 oriented products in that it includes more smaller-cap stocks. BetaShares offers an ETF that tracks the technology-heavy NASDAQ-100 index (NDQ). This index has shown good relative performance in recent years.

BetaShares also offers a fundamentally weighted US ETF (QUS) which – like its Australian counterpart, QOZ – aims to outperform traditional market-cap weighted indices.   This is by effectively reducing the weight it attaches to stocks that are highly priced relative to other fundamental measures (such as earnings and book value), and hence more likely to suffer a price correction. UBS also offers yet another ethical product, this time focused on the US market.

Another interesting option is the "wide moat" ETF offered by VanEck Vectors. This ETF aims to track a rules-based index comprised of at least 40 "attractively priced wide moat" US stocks, as determined by Morningstar's "time-tested proprietary research." By "wide moat", these are stocks judged to have "sustainable competitive advantages".

Last, but not least, in this area is Vanguard's US Market Shares ETF, which tracks all stocks (by market cap) that trade on the New York Stock Exchange.

As such, the ETF covers large, mid, small and micro-cap stocks. The special feature of this ETF is that it is very cheap, with a management fee of only 0.05%!   A major reason for this cost advantage is that it is a cross-listed version of a much larger fund operated in the United States, and as a result does give rise to extra tax and administrative issues for Australian investors.

Bear and Gear Funds

As with the bear and gear funds that cover the Australian market, BetaShares has also made available funds which provide magnified or short exposure to the US market.

Through short positions in the S&P 500 futures contracts, the BetaShares US Equities Strong Bear Hedge Fund (ASX Code: BBUS) can be expected to deliver a gain on any given day of between 2.0% to 2.75% for every 1% *fall* in the U.S. share market (and vice versa). As for the Australian equity market Bear and Strong Bear Funds above, there is no need for investors to explicitly borrow funds, as this is managed internally within BBUS's structure. Thus, investors are not exposed to margin calls.

Similarly, BetaShares also offers a geared US equity fund (ASX Code: GGUS) which can be expected to deliver a gain on any given day of between 2.0% to 2.75% for every 1% *rise* in the U.S. share market (and vice versa).   The Fund can also borrow on professional *wholesale* markets at considerably cheaper rates than typically available to a retail investor.

Note both BBUS and GGUS are also currency hedged.

ASIAN EQUITY ETFS

The range of Asian equity ETFs is also growing. As seen in the table below, investors have the choice of having broad Asian regional equity exposure or more specific country exposures.

The iShares S&P Asia 50 ETF, for example, provides exposure to the top 50 companies across Hong Hong (including Hong Kong-listed Chinese companies), South Korea, Singapore and Hong Kong. UBS's "ethical" offering provides essentially similar regional exposure to that of iShares, but again excludes companies exposed to tobacco or "controversial" weapons.

Compared to iShares and UBS, Vanguard's FTSE Asia ex-Japan ETF has a somewhat lower Chinese concentration, which is offset with more exposure to India and smaller economies, such as Malaysia and Indonesia.

Asian Equity Based ETPs as at Dec 2015*						
ASX Code	Product Type	Fund Name	ICR (%p.a.)*	FUM ($m)	# trades	Bid-Offer % spread
Regional						
IAA	ETF	iShares S&P Asia 50	0.50	$260.0	663	0.29%
UBP	ETF	UBS IQ MSCI Asia APEX 50 Ethical ETF	0.45	$0.9	3	0.38%
VAE	ETF	Vanguard FTSE Asia Ex-Japan Shares Index ETF	0.40	$23.1	16	n/a
Japan						
IJP	ETF	iShares MSCI Japan	0.48	$207.8	662	0.28%
UBJ	ETF	UBS IQ MSCI Japan Ethical ETF	0.40	$3.1	26	0.26%
HJPN	ETF	Betashares WisdomTree Japan ETF – Currency Hedged	0.58	-	-	-
China/Hong Kong						
IZZ	ETF	iShares FTSE China Large-Cap	0.74	$82.3	294	0.33%
CETF	ETF	Market Vectors ChinaAMC A-Share ETF (Synthetic)	0.72	$2.4	40	0.48%
IHK	ETF	iShares MSCI Hong Kong	0.48	$15.1	41	0.47%
Other						
IKO	ETF	iShares MSCI South Korea Capped Index	0.62	$15.4	150	0.47%
ISG	ETF	iShares MSCI Singapore	0.48	$8.9	22	0.50%
ITW	ETF	iShares MSCI Taiwan	0.62	$39.3	191	0.44%

*HJPN since May 2016

Japan is also catered for, with a specific country ETF provided by iShares and BetaShares, and an "ethical" variant provided by UBS. The BetaShares ETF (HJPN) is currency hedged and also locally domiciled.

Mainland Chinese companies are available through two ETFs. iShares' IZZ tracks Chinese "H-shares" or mainland Chinese companies listed on the Hong Kong Stock Exchange (and so, generally available to foreign investors), while the product provided by VanEck Vectors tracks so-called "A-shares," or companies listed on the Shenzhen or Shanghai Stock Exchange. The latter stocks are not generally open to foreign investment, but can be accessed through specialised funds authorised by the Chinese Government.

One issue with Chinese H-shares vs. A-shares is valuation. As the Chinese A-market is relatively more closed, it is dominated by the whims of retail investors and company valuations are generally higher than for H-shares on the more competitive Hong Kong Exchange. Either way, investors are advised to have a sense of the relative valuations across each market before opting for one ETF over the other. Other Asian ETFs cater specifically to the Hong Kong, South Korean, Singaporean, and Taiwanese markets.

EUROPE

The European Equity market is also covered by four ETPs – from iShares, Vanguard, BetaShares and an "ethical" variant from UBS. European equity exposure (along with that in Japan) was a popular global theme in 2015, based on the belief that these markets are relatively less expensive than that of the United States, and their economies might benefit from relatively low interest rates and weakening exchange rates over the next year or so.

European Equity Based ETPs as at Dec 2015						
ASX Code	Product Type	Fund Name	ICR (%p.a.)*	FUM ($m)	# trades	Bid-Offer % spread
IEU	ETF	iShares S&P Europe	0.60	$627.2	1,197	0.22%
UBE	ETF	UBS IQ MSCI Europe Ethical ETF	0.40	$7.4	17	0.34%
VEQ	ETF	Vanguard FTSE Europe Shares ETF	0.35	$3.0	17	0.67%
HEUR*	ETF	BetaShares Wisdom Tree Europe ETF-Currency Hedged	0.58	-	-	-

*Since May 2016

The iShares European ETF has been the longest established in the market and has retained the largest FUM at the end of 2015, $627m. Vanguard only recently entered this field, though it maintains a competitive expense fee of only 0.35%. All apart from the BetaShare's ETF are unhedged, meaning investors also need to take on board European currency risk when investing in either. The BetaShares ETF, HEUR, also has the tax and administrative advantages of being locally domiciled.

EMERGING MARKETS

Although accounting for approximately half of global output, emerging markets still account for only a little more than 10 per cent of global stock market capitalisation.

There are four ETPs that cover emerging markets as a group. iShares (IEM), Vanguard (VGE), and State Street (WEMG) all offer ETFs with broadly similar exposure across the emerging market group of countries – although only iShares includes South Korea in this group.

Investors can also choose a BRICs ETF, which only covers Brazil, Russia, India, and China (IBK) – thereby giving more weight to these emerging markets, while excluding other emerging markets, such as South Korea, Taiwan, South Africa, and Mexico - which are included in the broader IEM.

iShares' IEM has been on the local market longer, and so has built up the greatest support, with $336 million under management as of the end of 2015.   This ETF tracks the MSCI emerging markets equity index, which as of the end of 2015 had 26% exposure to China, with the next heaviest exposures to South Korea (15%) and Taiwan (12%).   Investors considering emerging markets might naturally think of commodity exporters, such as Brazil and Russia. But, it might surprise some to know that financials accounted for 28% of the MSCI Emerging Market Index as of the end of 2015, followed by a 21% share for information technology.

Compared to developed market ETFs, the bid-offer spreads for these ETFs are not bad considering the difficulties that market makers face in hedging their exposures given that many emerging markets don't trade during the Australian time zone.

Emerging Market Equity ETPs as at Dec 2015						
ASX Code	Product Type	Fund Name	ICR (%p.a.)*	FUM ($m)	# trades	Bid-Offer % spread
VGE	ETF	Vanguard FTSE Emerging Markets Shares ETF	0.48	$46.4	229	0.45%
WEMG	ETF	SPDR S&P Emerging Markets Fund	0.65	$6.4	22	0.39%
IBK	ETF	iShares MSCI BRIC	0.68	$33.8	243	0.57%
IEM	ETF	iShares MSCI Emerging Markets	0.68	$335.7	967	0.27%

Alternately, investors that prefer a stronger emerging markets *Asian* flavour can choose the Asia 50 ETF (IAA) referred to above, which includes only China, Hong Kong, South Korea, Taiwan, and Singapore (although Singapore is no longer defined as an emerging market). This naturally excludes non-Asian emerging economies, such as Russia, Brazil, and India.

Switching from the BRICs ETF to the Asia 50 ETF (IAA) effectively involves replacing Brazil, Russia, and India with South Korea, Taiwan, and Singapore. Both ETFs contain China and Hong Kong to a similar degree. As should be apparent, the choice between IAA and IBK in the emerging markets area is essentially between Asian technology plays (Korea and Taiwan), or commodity producers (Brazil and Russia).

If one can't decide between these areas, an investor might be better off sticking with the broadly diversified emerging markets ETFs, IEM, VGE, or WEMG. As noted above, iShares' emerging markets ETF (IEM) is among the more popular international ETFs across the market. The narrower IBK emerging markets option is not nearly as popular, with investors preferring the more Asian-focused alternatives of IAA or IZZ.

Unlike in the case of developed markets, emerging markets did tend to outperform the Australian market during the "commodity boom" over the decade prior to the global financial crisis (see chart below). This outperformance was less evident in unhedged $A terms, however, due to a weakness in emerging market currencies versus the stronger Australian dollar. Emerging markets have broadly underperformed since 2012, as commodity prices started to turn down. In the past year, emerging markets have been particularly hurt over fears of a rising US dollar.

Emerging market underperformance has not been as bad in unhedged terms against the Australian market in recent years due to a weakness in the $A (which in turn reflects $US strength, and the fact that several emerging markets peg their currency to the greenback).

EM vs. Australian Equity Performance

MSCI All Country Index vs S&P/ASX 200

Index Dec'95 = 100

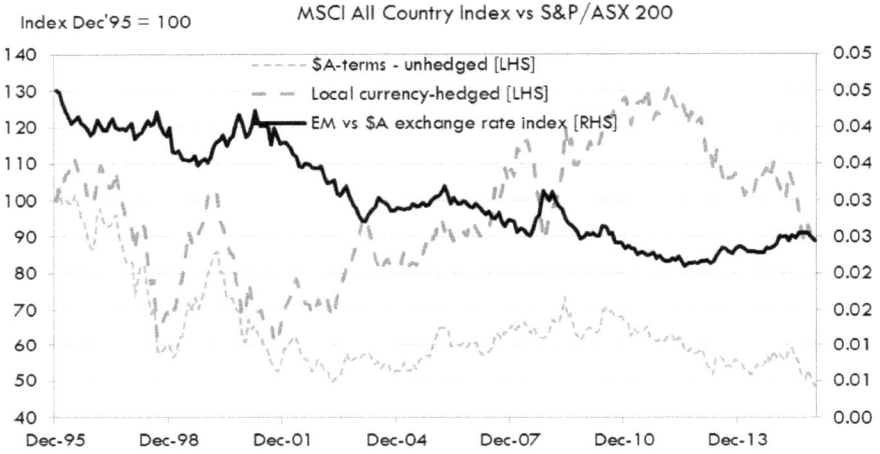

Source: Thomson Reuters

GLOBAL SECTOR ETFS

Last, but not least, another way to tap into global equity markets is from a sector-based perspective. As seen in the table below, iShares offers three (unhedged) global sector exposures covering the health care, consumer staples, and telecommunications sectors.

This can offer useful investment diversification for investors, given that the Australian equity market is relatively heavily weighted toward financial and resource stocks.

Global Equity Sector ETPs as at Dec 2015						
ASX Code	Product Type	Fund Name	ICR (%p.a.)*	FUM ($m)	# trades	Bid-Offer % spread
DJRE	ETF	SPDR Dow Jones Global Select Real Estate Fund	0.50	$75.2	325	0.22%
GDX	ETF	VanEck Vectors Gold Miners	0.53	$10.7	182	0.34%
IXI	ETF	iShares S&P Global Consumer	0.47	$151.5	326	0.30%
IXJ	ETF	iShares S&P Global Healthcare	0.47	$436.8	955	0.23%
IXP	ETF	iShares S&P Global Telecommunications	0.47	$23.1	98	0.50%

As seen in the chart below, the iShares global healthcare and consumer staples sector ETFs have provided relatively strong returns in recent years. This is partly currency related. But, these sectors have also outperformed the iShare's Global 100 ETF's strong returns in $A terms over this period.   The healthcare sector especially seems well placed to benefit from global population ageing and rising health demands over the next few decades.

Global Sector Performance to 31-Dec 2015

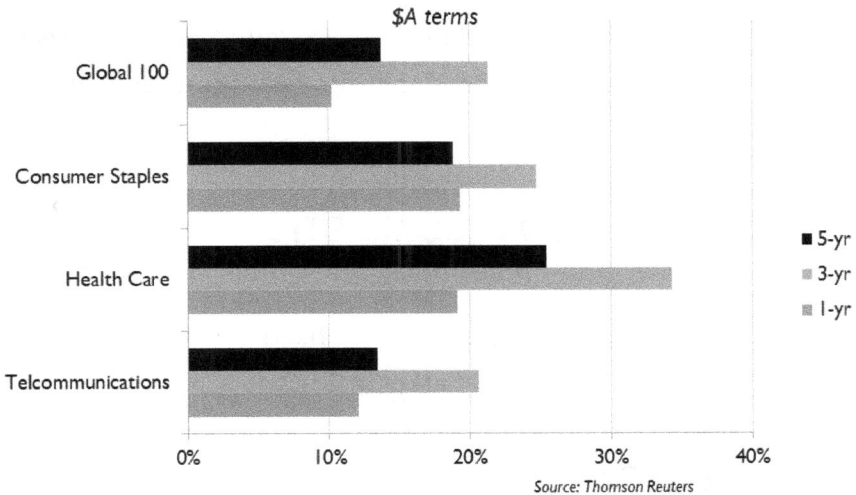

Source: Thomson Reuters

State Street also offers exposure to international property, while VanEck Vectors have ETFs covering global gold miners and infrastructure. The recently launched infrastructure offering, IFRA, is particularly innovative for the Australian market, covering a portfolio of listed infrastructure businesses across developed markets in the areas of transportation, energy and telecommunications. This ETF is also 50% currency hedged.

While on the subject of sectors, moreover, it's worth remembering that BetaShares offers good access to the technology sector – largely via US firms, but also through some global names - through the NASDAQ 100 index. Indeed, the NASDAQ-100 is effectively like a sector ETF given that – as of the end of 2015 – technology stocks comprised 55% of the index. Consumer discretionary and health care stocks accounted for a further 20% and 15% of the index, respectively. In terms of diversification, it's noteworthy that technology, health care, and consumer discretionary stocks have a relatively low weight in the Australian market, given the latter is dominated by financial and resource stocks.

Over July and August 2016, BetaShares also launched global sector ETFs covering the banking, gold mining, healthcare and internet security sectors.

AUSTRALIAN FIXED INCOME ETFS

Adding to the asset allocation picture, fixed income ETFs were introduced into the Australian market in 2012.

BOND MARKET BASICS

Fixed income ETFs generate their returns by holding a benchmark selection of bonds. The return each year is a function of both the starting market yield being offered on the selection of bonds held, together with the change in the market price of the bonds due to changes in the interest rate.

The yield return on a given fixed income index is best measured by the *yield to maturity* (YTM), which equals the annual yield investors would receive were all bonds in the index held until maturation.

There are two main sources of risk in the fixed income market. Firstly, there is interest rate or "duration" risk. This risk arises because an increase in interest rates reduces the market value of fixed-coupon rate bonds, meaning that the returns that year will be below the starting yield offered on the bonds. By contrast, a fall in interest rates boosts the market value of these bonds, meaning that returns in any given year will be higher than the starting yield offered on the bonds.

As seen in the chart below, this means that the return on fixed income investments – especially over the short-term when capital returns can matter as much as income – is typically inversely related to interest rate changes. Falling interest rates are usually good for fixed-income returns, and vice-versa.

Bonds Returns vs Interest Rates
1990-2015

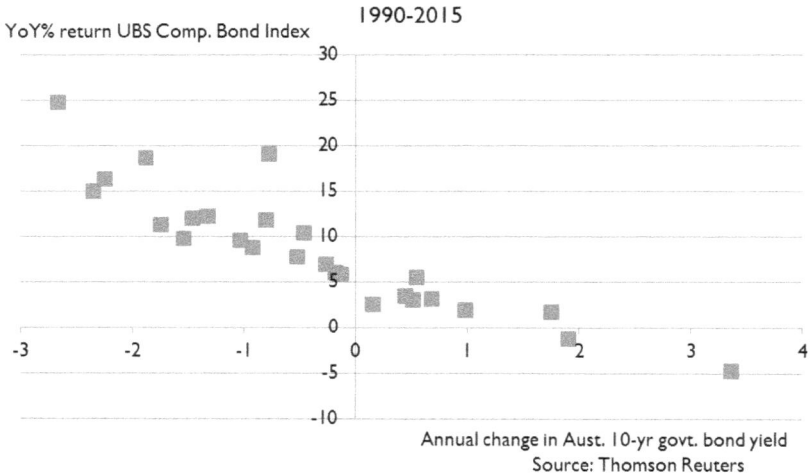

YoY% return UBS Comp. Bond Index

Annual change in Aust. 10-yr govt. bond yield
Source: Thomson Reuters

All else equal, the more years to a bond's maturity (or duration), the more sensitive is its current market value to changes in interest rates. This means that there is greater price volatility risk, for which investors usually expect a higher yield in compensation.

A second source of risk is credit risk, which reflects the risk that bond issuers may eventually default on paying back interest rate capital when due. Again, the greater the credit risk, the greater the yield investors can expect. One objective measure of credit risk is the credit rating that agencies, such as Moody's and Standard & Poor's, attach to bonds. The following credit ratings table is from Vanguard.

Moody's and Standard & Poor's bond-rating codes

	Moody's	S&P	Rating
Investment-Grade Bonds	Aaa	AAA	Highest quality with lowest risk; issuers are exceptionally stable and dependable.
	Aa	AA	High quality, slightly higher degree of long-term risk.
	A	A	High-medium quality, many strong attributes but somewhat vulnerable to changing economic conditions.
	Baa	BBB	Medium quality, adequate but less reliable over the long term.
Below Investment-Grade Bonds	Ba	BB	Somewhat speculative, moderate security but not well safeguarded.
	B	B	Low quality, future default risk.
	Caa	CCC	Poor quality, clear danger of default.
	Ca	CC	Highly speculative, often in default.
	C	C	Lowest rating, poor prospects of repayment.
		D	In default.

Sources: Standard & Poor's and Moody's Investors Service.

In Australia, the credit risk spectrum moves from Federal (Australian) Government bonds being the safest (triple A-rated), to State Government bonds (generally, double A) and then to corporate (mainly, bank) bonds, with ratings that are generally only slightly below State Governments' ratings.

BLOOMBERG COMPOSITE AUSTRALIAN BOND INDEX

The Australian key domestic fixed-income benchmark is the Bloomberg Composite Australian Bond Index, which includes both Government and corporate bonds. This is the main benchmark against which active fixed-income fund managers typically assess their performance.

As of the end of 2015, the Bloomberg Composite Australian Bond Index included approximately half Federal Government bonds, one quarter State Government bonds, 15 per cent locally issued international governmental agencies bonds, and around 10 per cent corporate bonds (of which bank bonds account for one-half).

Bloomberg Composite Bond Index - Dec 2015

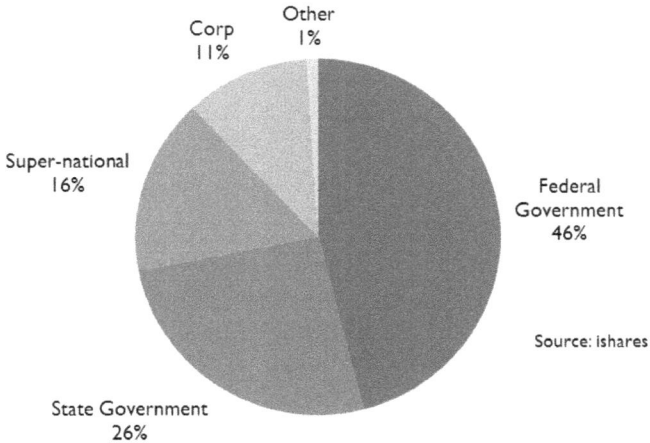

Corp 11%
Other 1%
Super-national 16%
Federal Government 46%
Source: ishares
State Government 26%

Using this index as the benchmark, it should be noted that fixed income return volatility is usually considerably less than that of equities. Due to this lower "risk," long-run fixed income returns are typically less than that for equities.

For example, in the 12 years until the end of 2015, the Bloomberg Australian Bond Composite Index provided a compound annualised return of 6.2%, compared with an 8.7% annualised return from the S&P/ASX 200 equity index. However, there were no negative annual returns for the bond index over this period, with gains ranging from 1.7% in 2009 (as interest rates rebounded following the global financial crisis) to 14.9% a year earlier, when interest rates had plummeted. By contrast, Australian equities suffered a total return loss of 38.4% in 2008, with the strongest gain being 24.2% in 2006.

The other notable feature is that the returns on bonds and equities are usually negatively correlated – especially in the last few decades of aggressive counter-cyclical central bank actions.

For example, weak economic growth hurts corporate earnings, but may also cause the central bank to cut interest rates if inflation also falls. This boosts fixed income returns, at the same time that equity returns are poor. When the economy picks up, however, central banks raise interest rates again while corporate earnings recover. This means that fixed income returns are hurt, while equities perform well. Over the past 12 years until the end of 2015, the correlation between annual returns from the Australian bond and equity indices mentioned above was minus 0.77.

The low correlation between equity and bonds returns - and the relatively low volatility of fixed income returns outright - means fixed income investments are useful sources of diversification for investment portfolios, complementing equity holdings. By adding some fixed income investments to a portfolio, it may be possible to reduce overall portfolio risk without greatly sacrificing investment returns.

BOND MARKET ETFS

As specified in the table below, investors have some choices in terms of the risk and returns that they want from fixed-income ETFs. Some ETFs only invest in Federal Government bonds (IGB and RGB), others only in State Government bonds (RSM), Federal and State Government bonds combined (GOVT, ILB, and VGB), only corporate bonds (RCB), or Federal, State, and corporate bonds combined (BOND, IAF, and VAF). ILB, moreover, only invests in *inflation-indexed* State and Federal Government bonds.

Australian Fixed Income ETPs as at Dec 2015						
ASX Code	Product Type	Fund Name	ICR (%p.a.)*	FUM ($m)	# trades	Bid-Offer % spread
Composite (Federal, State and Corporate Bonds)						
VAF	ETF	Vanguard Australian Fixed Interest Index ETF	0.20	$316.7	1,120	0.13%
IAF	ETF	iShares Composite Bond ETF	0.24	$267.7	587	0.20%
BOND	ETF	SPDR S&P/ASX Australian Bond Fund	0.24	$20.8	78	0.17%
Federal Government Bonds						
IGB	ETF	iShares Treasury ETF	0.26	$18.2	82	0.30%
RGB	ETF	Russell Australian Government Bond ETF	0.24	$165.3	32	0.39%
State Government Bonds						
RSM	ETF	Russell Australian Semi-Government Bond ETF	0.26	$94.1	69	0.38%
Federal & State Government Bonds						
ILB	ETF	iShares Government Inflation Index Fund	0.26	$51.8	160	0.38%
GOVT	ETF	SPDR S&P/ASX Australian Government Bond Fund	0.22	$7.7	27	0.16%
VGB	ETF	Vanguard Australian Governnment Bond Index ETF	0.20	$67.2	202	0.31%
Corporate Bond Index						
RCB	ETF	Russell Australian Select Corporate Bond ETF	0.28	$72.6	216	0.28%

As might be expected, the more popular fixed income ETFs as of the end of 2015 were those that provided broad fixed income exposure – across Government and corporate bonds.

Both the iShares and Vanguard ETFs (IAF and VAF), for example, track the industry benchmark Bloomberg Australian Composite Bond Index. State Street have their own broad fixed income index, which is broadly similar in allocation among Federal, State, and Corporate Bonds.

The relationship between yield to maturity and duration for the Australian bond indices and the ETFs that track them is illustrated in the chart below, which is based on the prevailing interest rates as of the end of 2015.

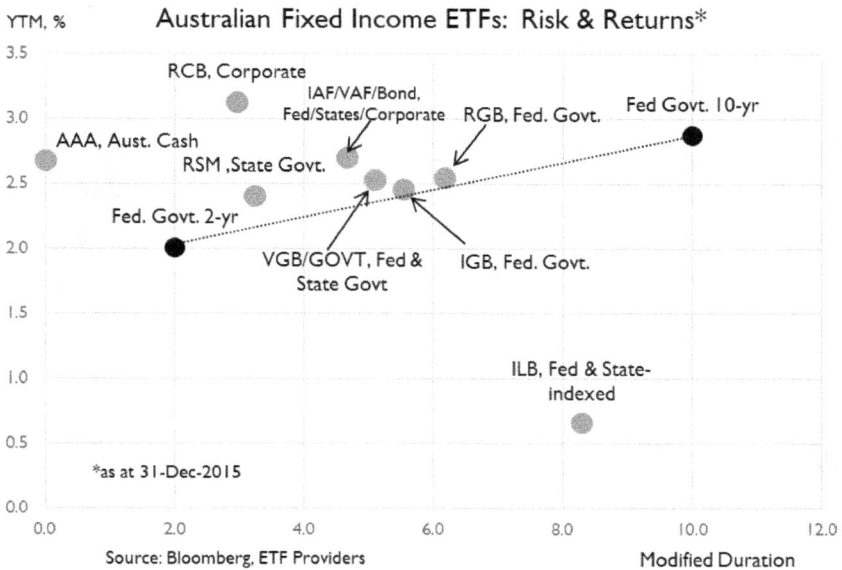

Australian Fixed Income ETFs: Risk & Returns*

YTM, %

RCB, Corporate
IAF/VAF/Bond, Fed/States/Corporate
RGB, Fed. Govt.
Fed Govt. 10-yr
AAA, Aust. Cash
RSM ,State Govt.
Fed. Govt. 2-yr
VGB/GOVT, Fed & State Govt
IGB, Fed. Govt.
ILB, Fed & State-indexed

*as at 31-Dec-2015

Source: Bloomberg, ETF Providers

Modified Duration

Indeed, as a benchmark of prevailing interest rates, the chart above also includes the market yields on offer for Australian Federal Government 2-year and 10-year bonds at the time.

Two features should be immediately apparent. As suggested above, there is generally an inverse relationship between the average duration of bonds in an index and the index's yield to maturity. There is also a positive correlation between yield and credit risk – with indices that contain some or all corporate bonds generally offering higher yields for a given duration. For example, Russell Investment's pure corporate bond ETF (RCB) offers a relatively high yield-to-maturity of 3%, compared with just over 2% for its State Government bond ETF (RSM), even though the average duration of both bonds in the former ETF was slightly *lower* than in the latter.

These risk relationships suggest that if the provided interest rate spreads between these bond types remain constant, investments in corporate bonds will usually produce a higher long-run return than those in State Government bonds, which in turn will produce higher returns than those for Federal Government bonds.

Also noteworthy is the very low yield for iShare's inflation-indexed bond, ETF (ILB). These bonds also make a separate regular capital value adjustment to compensate for rising inflation. If consumer prices rise 5% in a year, for example, the capital value of indexed bonds also increase 5%. Therefore, the "real value" of one's investment is not eroded over time by inflation. As a result, the interest rate paid is effectively a *real* yield. Unlike in the case of non-indexed bonds, investors do not need to demand an added inflation premium on top of the interest rate.

Last, but not least, also included in the chart above is the BetaShares Australian High Interest Cash ETF (AAA), which essentially invests in bank term deposits. Given the very low yields now on offer in the fixed income market, the yield on the AAA is relatively attractive – especially given that it has effectively zero duration or interest rate risk, as the market value of this investment (unlike for bonds) is not sensitive to overall interest rate changes.

CORPORATE BOND RISK AND RETURN

While corporate bonds generally offer higher yields than Government bonds (for the same maturity), the *volatility* in returns actually tends to be a bit less than for Government bonds. This odd feature reflects two factors:

First, owing to the lack of depth in the local corporate bond market, corporate bonds on issue tend to have *shorter maturity* than Government bonds. This dampens the sensitivity of their returns to interest rate changes relative to that of longer-dated Government bond indices. The bonds in the corporate bond index tracked by Russell's RCB, for example, have an average remaining term to maturity of around 3.3 years, compared with 5.2 years for Federal Government bonds in the index tracked by iShare's IGB.

A second factor is the typically counter-cyclical movement in risk spreads within the fixed-income market. In times of economic weakness when interest rates are falling and bond returns are high, interest rates on corporate and State Government bonds usually fall by *less* than those for Federal Government bonds (interest rate risk spreads rise), meaning the (capital) gains on the former bonds in a falling interest rate environment are not as significant as for Federal Government bonds.

When economic growth recovers, however, interest rates on corporate and State Government bonds don't rise as much as for Federal Government bonds. The risk spread narrows again, meaning that the former bonds tend to outperform Federal Government bonds.

Corporate bond returns, for example, did not rise by as much as Federal Government bond returns when interest rates fell during the 2008 global financial crisis. Corporate bond returns then did not *fall* as much as interest rates rose during 2009. This also means that corporate bond returns are not as negatively correlated with equity market returns as those of Government bonds (history over the past decade or so, however, shows that the overall correlation is still significantly negative).

Less active longer-term investors might prefer to simply buy and hold an ETF covering a broad index of Federal, State, and corporate bonds. That said some investors might prefer to earn relatively higher long-run returns (with less return volatility) by investing in fixed income ETFs that are more narrowly focused on corporate bonds only.

One word of caution, however, is needed for those prepared to take on added corporate risk for higher returns. As illustrated in the chart below, yield spreads for owning semi-government or corporate bonds rather than Federal Government bonds had shrunk to relatively low levels by the end of 2015 – as investors chased yield in a relatively low global interest rate environment. This suggests that there's now relatively little extra risk compensation for holding these broader bond indices compared with the Treasury bond index alone. Should there be another financial crisis or global recession, these bond spreads are likely to widen – meaning higher risk corporate and semi-government bonds will underperform Federal Government bond returns.

Investors should note that unlike in the United States, Australia's corporate bond market is relatively small and is dominated by offerings from (relatively safe) major banks. As a result, there is not the choice of higher yield/higher risk bonds as we'll see later with international fixed-income ETFs.

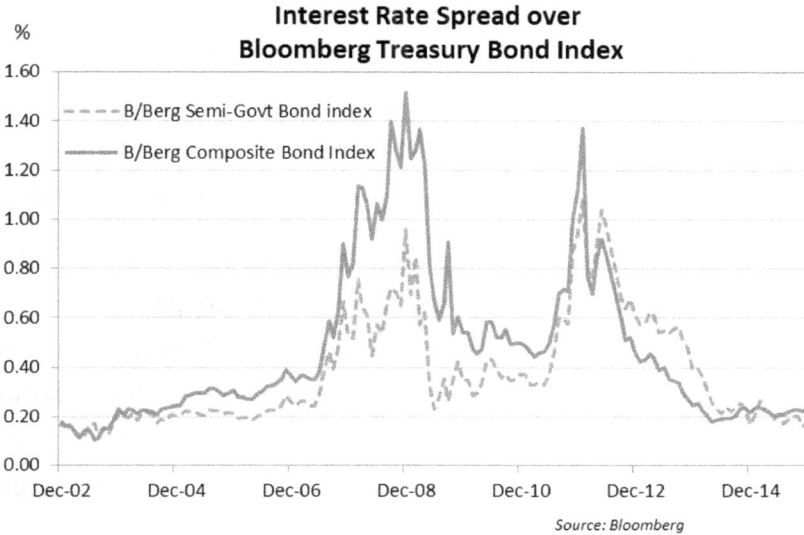

Interest Rate Spread over Bloomberg Treasury Bond Index

Source: Bloomberg

INDEXED BOND ETFs

A special word should be added on the inflation-indexed fixed income ETF.

As noted above, the yield on this ETF is less than that on non-indexed government bonds, as investors in the latter demand a higher yield to compensate for the lack of inflation indexation. The yield difference between non-indexed and indexed government bonds can be considered an estimate of the market's future long-term inflation expectation – less a slight "liquidity" premium for non-inflation indexed bonds due to their greater quantity and generally higher market liquidity, especially in times of crisis.

In this regard, it should be noted that indexed bond ETFs do not *necessarily* provide better inflation protection than non-indexed bond ETFs over time – it depends on the inflation expectations embedded in nominal yields at the time of purchase.

If the average yield on non-indexed bonds was 6% and that on indexed bonds was 3.5%, for example, the market could be considered to anticipate inflation of 2.5% over the term of these bonds. If inflation *did* average 2.5%, the return on both indexed and non-indexed bonds over this period would be effectively the same.

However, if inflation ended up being *higher* than the market's current 2.5% expectation, investors in the indexed product would end up better off. However, they'd be worse off if inflation turned out lower than expected. In this sense, the inflation indexed bonds guard against the risk of much higher than *currently expected* inflation. Indexed bonds are a less compelling hedge against future inflation if the market is already pricing in a lot of potential inflation through, say, unusually high nominal bond yields.

As of the end of 2015, the yield differential between indexed and non-indexed bonds – the market's implied inflation expectation – had dropped to approximately 2%, or the lower edge of the Reserve Bank of Australia's (RBA) 2 to 3 per cent inflation target band. That suggests a relatively small compensation for inflation risk, given that the RBA is likely to try to avoid inflation dropping lower than 2 per cent for an extended period. This would presently favour investments in indexed rather than non-indexed bonds, especially if one fears that inflation will average more than 2 per cent over the coming decade or so.

Implied Market Inflation Expectation

Yield difference between the UBS Non-indexed and Indexed Government Bond Index

%

Source: Bloomberg

Either way, investing in the indexed fixed income ETF might suit investors who were particularly worried about upside surprises in the inflation outlook. As with corporate and State Government interest rate spreads, shifts in the market's implied inflation expectation over time may present tactical switching opportunities for more active fixed-income investors.

For example, the non-indexed government bond benchmark is likely to outperform the indexed benchmark for a time if the market's implied inflation expectation is unreasonably high (i.e. interest rates on nominal bonds were relatively high compared to those on indexed bonds), as was last seen in mid-2008. The reverse is true when the market's inflation expectation is especially low, as was last seen in mid-2009 (and potentially again in late 2013).

As noted above, the yield difference between indexed and non-indexed bonds does not just reflect inflation expectations, but also a "liquidity premium" attached to non-indexed bonds (given that they are in much greater supply and have more market depth). In times of high financial stress, non-indexed government bond yields are likely to drop by more than indexed bond yields, effectively reducing the market's implied long-term inflation expectation. Either way, such pricing extremes may present opportunities to switch between indexed and non-indexed bond ETFs.

INTERNATIONAL BOND ETFS

One of the more recent additions to the local ETP market is international fixed income products, offered by iShares and Vanguard. As seen in the table below, there were five international fixed income ETFs on the market as of the end of 2015. Given that they are relatively new to the market, they only have a small amount of funds under management. All these ETFs are also currency hedged, meaning investors assume no currency risk.

International Fixed Income ETPs as at Dec 2015						
ASX Code	Product Type	Fund Name	ICR (%p.a.)*	FUM ($m)	# trades	Bid-Offer % spread
VIF	ETF	Vanguard International Fixed Interest Index (Hedged) ETF	0.20	$2.0	31	0.40%
VCF	ETF	Vanguard International Credit Securities Index (Hedged) ETF	0.30	$1.0	19	0.43%
IHCB	ETF	iShares Global Corporate Bond (AUD Hedged) ETF	0.26	$2.0	2	0.41%
IHEB	ETF	iShares J.P.Morgan USD Emerging Markets Bond (AUD Hedged) ETF	0.52	$1.0	3	0.41%
IHHY	ETF	iShares Global High Yield Bond (AUD Hedged) ETF	0.56	$1.9	3	0.41%

Vanguard provides exposure to developed market national government bonds (such as those of the US, Japan, and European countries) through VIF, which is the least credit risky (at least according to the rating agencies!) and lowest yielding offerings in this space.   Vanguard's VCF offers a slightly riskier and better yielding collection of corporate and government-related (i.e., issued by national and international governmental agencies) bonds.

Even higher risk and return offerings are provided by iShares, through a pure global corporate bond ETF (IHCB), an emerging market sovereign and quasi-sovereign bond ETF (IHEB), and a high-yield corporate bond ETF (IHHY).

In terms of credit ratings, and therefore credit risk, IHHY has the highest risk among these iShares ETFs (with bonds that generally have a BB or B rating, which is below "investment grade"), while bonds in the IHCB have a higher investment grade rating (A or BBB).   IHEB's credit risk is somewhere in between, with credit ratings in the BBB to BB range.

The chart below details the duration and yield characteristics of these different international bond ETFs as of the end of 2015.

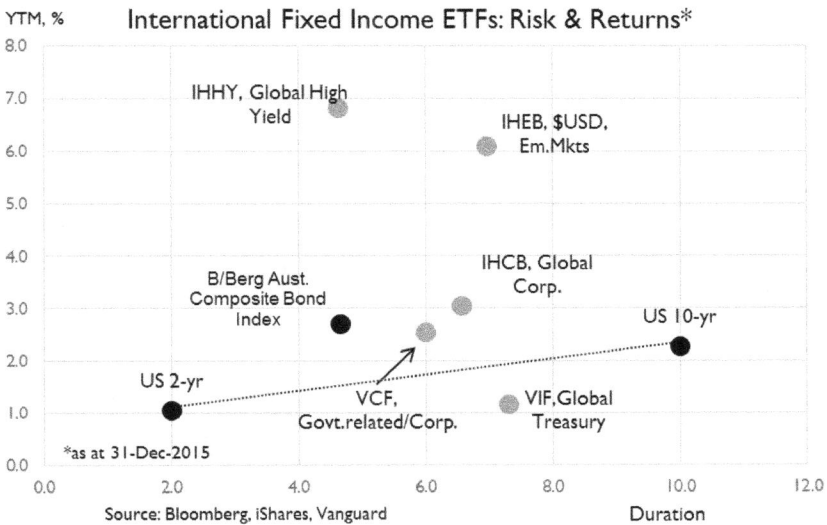

International Fixed Income ETFs: Risk & Returns*

YTM, %

- 8.0
- 7.0   IHHY, Global High Yield
- 6.0   IHEB, $USD, Em.Mkts
- 5.0
- 4.0   IHCB, Global Corp.
- 3.0   B/Berg Aust. Composite Bond Index   US 10-yr
- 2.0
- 1.0   US 2-yr   VCF, Govt.related/Corp.   VIF,Global Treasury
- 0.0   *as at 31-Dec-2015

Duration: 0.0   2.0   4.0   6.0   8.0   10.0   12.0

Source: Bloomberg, iShares, Vanguard

Also included, for the sake of comparison, is the yield and duration for US 2-year and 10-year Treasury Bonds, as well as for the Bloomberg Australian Composite Bond index.

The credit risk priced into iShares IHHY and IHEB is evident from the fact that the yields-to-maturity they offer are quite high relative to IHCB and VCF for comparable duration risks. So, even in today's "low yield environment," reasonably attractive currency-hedged yields are available in the international fixed-income space for investors prepared to take on associated credit risks. Again, risk in this case is that of capital losses should higher risk corporate and emerging market interest rates surge due, say, to another financial crisis.

As demonstrated by the chart below, at the end of 2015, global credit spreads had risen from unusually low levels and so were offering reasonable value. That said, spreads were still below the peak levels evident during US economic recessions or broader financial panics, so it remained a case of "buyer beware."

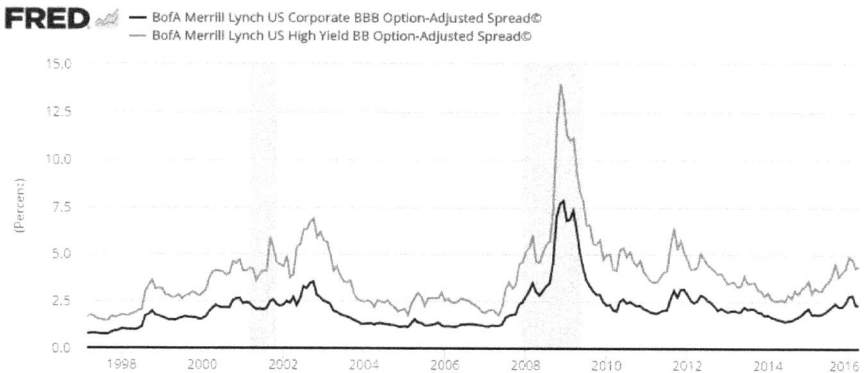

While core international fixed income exposure (such as through VIF) can offer *some* portfolio diversification benefits for investors, as seen in the chart below, the returns on such a benchmark have tended to be highly correlated with those from the domestic fixed income market – as global bonds yields tend to move closely together. That was especially the case in the 1990s when inflation and interest rates fell in tandem across the globe.

Australian vs. International Annual Bond Returns

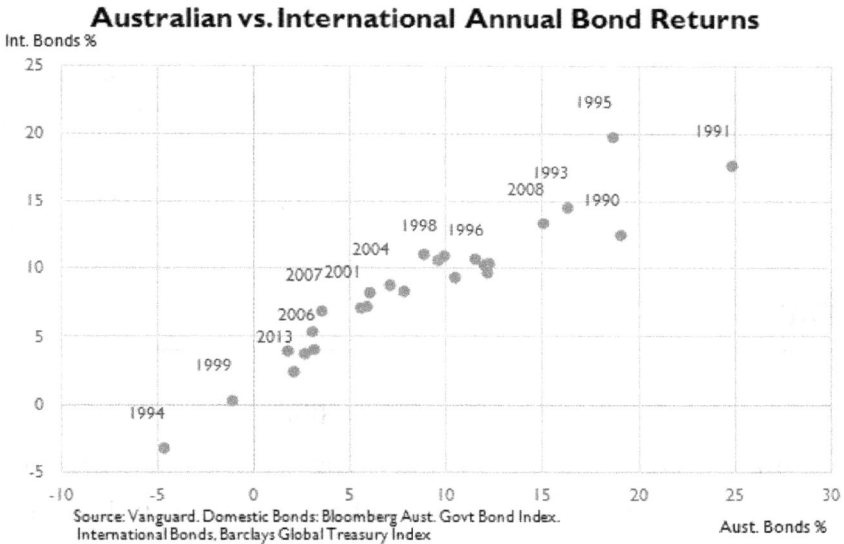

Source: Vanguard. Domestic Bonds: Bloomberg Aust. Govt Bond Index.
International Bonds, Barclays Global Treasury Index

CASH ETFS

In what is perhaps the simplest ETF conceivable, but one that has proven to be very popular, BetaShares offers a cash-based ETF (ASX Code: AAA) which invests in high-yield bank deposits.

This allows investors, should they so desire, to keep all their funds in ASX-traded investments, held through a single equity broker account, which might be much cheaper than investing through, say, an investment platform. There are no ongoing annual "platform" fees from holding ASX-traded investments through a simple share trading account. What's more AAA has, since its inception at least, provided interest returns of approximately 0.25% to 0.5% more than the average bank term deposit of between one and six months, all while providing ready access to funds if needed. As highlighted above, the AAA yield, as of the end of 2015, seemed attractive compared with those available on Australian longer-maturity fixed-income ETFs.

Cash ETPs as at Dec 2015						
ASX Code	Product Type	Fund Name	ICR (%p.a.)*	FUM ($m)	# trades	Bid-Offer % spread
AAA	ETF	BetaShares Australian High Interest Cash ETF	0.18	$792.8	1,818	0.02%

COMMODITY ETPS

Investors also have a range of commodity ETPs to choose from, covering precious metals, energy, and agricultural products. Investors can also choose to invest in broad commodity indices, or more specific markets, like gold or oil.

For long-term investors, commodity ETPs are seen as a useful investment diversification option, especially in a rising inflation environment (such as in the 1970s), in which bonds and equities both performed poorly. Fear of inflation - due to central banks printing money - has been a major factor underpinning the popularity of gold ETPs in recent years.

Up until mid-2011, there had been fairly broad-based global commodity price gains for almost a decade - due to rising demand from emerging countries, such as China, and a slow supply-side response. Since then, price performance has not been as great, due to both increased supply (in response to earlier high prices) and a slowdown in China's growth in demand.

ASX Code	Product Type	Fund Name	ICR (%p.a.)*	FUM ($m)	# trades	Bid-Offer % spread
Commodity ETPs as at Dec 2015*						
Broad Commodity						
QCB	ETF	BetaShares Commodities Basket ETF-Currency Hedged (Synthetic)	0.69	$7.8	8	0.84%
Precious Metals						
ETPMPM	SP	ETFS Precious Metals Basket	0.43	$4.2	3	0.81%
GOLD	Share	ETFS Physical Gold	0.40	$386.3	1,532	0.10%
PMGOLD	SP	Perth Mint Gold	0.15	$79.5	92	0.60%
QAU	ETF	BetaShares Gold Bullion ETF (AU$ Hedged)	0.59	$16.7	67	0.31%
ETPMPT	SP	ETFS Physical Platinum	0.49	$3.0	5	0.58%
ETPMAG	SP	ETFS Physical Silver	0.49	$41.4	149	0.66%
ETPMPD	SP	ETFS Physical Palladium	0.49	$0.7	2	0.80%
ZGOL	ETF	ANZ ETFS Physical Gold ETF	0.40	$0.7	13	n/a
Energy						
OOO	ETF	BetaShares Crude Oil Index ETF-Currency Hedged (Synthetic)	0.69	$30.9	518	0.20%
Agriculture						
QAG	ETF	BetaShares Agriculture ETF-Currency Hedged (Synthetic)	0.69	$2.6	10	0.58%

*Table has been ammended to reflect some ETF closures in March 2016

ETF = Exchange Traded Fund, SP = Structured Product, Share = Redeemable Preference Share

Exchange traded commodity products come in a more diverse range of structures than traditional physical replication ETFs. This means that investors need to understand what they are buying. Compared with equity markets, commodity price changes may be particularly volatile. This means that there are rewards if you get the timing right, but added risks if you do not.

BROAD COMMODITY ETPS

For those seeking broad commodity exposure, the BetaShares Commodity Basket ETF (QCB) tracks 24 commodities covering energy, metals, agricultural, and livestock.   This is a currency-hedged fund, and it is structured as an ETF. For practical purposes, the Fund holds exposure to all commodity markets through futures contracts – hence, its label as a "synthetic" ETF.

GOLD ETFS

By far the most popular commodity ETPs to date are gold ETFs, with the ETF Securities GOLD product - launched much earlier than its competitors - having the most funds under management, $387 million as of the end of 2015.

GOLD is actually structured as a redeemable preference share, rather than as a traditional physical asset backed ETF. However, since these shares also give investors rights to a 100 per cent gold-backed "bare trust" in their name, their security remains fairly high.

The Perth Mint has a gold fund with $79m FUM as of the end of 2015 (PMGOLD). It is labelled a "structured product," since it is based on a fully paid call option for one-hundredth of a troy ounce of physical gold. The investment is effectively back by the State West Australian Government. Another feature of this product is that the PMGOLD holding can be physically redeemed for any of the Perth Mint's bullion coins and bars.

BetaShares gold ETF (QAU), by contrast, is structured as a traditional *physically-replicated ETF,* with $17m FUM as of the end of 2015. ANZ also launched a gold ETF toward the end of 2015. As ETFs, these Funds invest their proceeds in physical gold bullion held in secure vaults around the world. Access to these vaults is controlled by independent third-party custodians.

The gold ETF run by BetaShares also has the added feature of being the only gold product that is $A currency hedged. This allows investors' gold exposure to more directly track the $US price of gold in global markets, without the added complication of currency fluctuations. Without hedging, for example, if the $US price of gold rises, the returns for an Australian investor may be offset to the extent that the $A also rises ($US falls). This is noteworthy given that $US gold prices and the $A tend to be positively correlated over time.

Given that Australian interest rates are also typically higher than those seen in the United States, the process of hedging (which is equivalent to borrowing $US dollars and using the proceeds to invest in $A dollars) effectively produces some net-interest income for investors.

Of course, if the $A falls at the same time that the $US price of gold rises, investors would have been better off – at least in this example – with *unhedged* exposure to gold. The net-income from hedging would also decrease (and possibly turn negative) if Australian interest rates fell relative to those seen in the United States.

After a strong run over the previous decade, gold prices have corrected themselves in recent years, and flows into gold ETFs have been partly reversed. In inflation adjusted terms, gold prices remain high relative to historical standards. Gold might still be valued for its "diversification" qualities, but the strong price uptrend may be over (at least for the foreseeable future).

Spot Gold Price

$ per ounce

Source: Thomson Reuters

OTHER COMMODITY ETPS

There is also a range of other commodity ETPs to meet most investors' needs in this space.

In the precious metals area, there are products that cover silver, platinum, and palladium. These products are also offered by ETF Securities and, similar to GOLD, are structured as redeemable preference shares.   At $41m, the silver ETP (ETPMAG) had the third highest FUM in the commodity space at the end of 2015, following only GOLD and PMGOLD.

The BetaShares Crude Oil Index ETF (OOO) is also among the more popular non-gold commodity ETPs with $31m FUM as of the end of 2015.   Last, but not least, BetaShares offers broad exposure to agricultural markets – corn, wheat, soybeans, and sugar - through QAG.

In the case of the BetaShares energy and agricultural ETPs, all are currency hedged and structured as synthetic ETFs, given the need for exposure via commodity futures contracts.

SYNTHETIC ETFS VS STRUCTURED PRODUCTS

As detailed above, other than for some gold products, most commodity ETPs need to use derivative contracts (such as swaps and futures) to obtain exposure to the underlying commodities. This is because it is not physically or practically possible to store, for example, barrels of oil, or have bags of wheat in the basement in the Sydney CBD!

Although necessary, use of derivatives can still generate investor concerns over security and risks.

The key concern with commodity ETPs (in this regard) is *counterparty risk* – or the risk that a portion of the net asset value of the Fund may be at risk, due to the failure of a derivative contract with the counterparty. Product issuers may beg to differ, but a reasonably broad rule of thumb is that *synthetic ETFs* have less counterparty risk (and generally better overall security) than a *structured product*. Among structured products, *collateralised products* have less counterparty risk than *synthetic structured products*.

As explained in Section 1, even though both may use derivatives, a key difference between synthetic ETFs and structured products is that the former must be run as a managed investment scheme or MIS. An MIS pools investor funds and must meet certain regulatory requirements in the interests of investor protection.

Synthetic ETFs, moreover, also can't allow the degree of counterparty exposure not backed by cash to exceed 10% of the

ETF's net asset value. This aims to ensure that if the counterparty goes bust overnight, investors are at most exposed to a 10% loss on their investment. In practice, ETF issuers manage their exposure to significantly less than 10%. What's more, the ASX requires that counterparties must meet certain requirements, which typically means they should either be a local or foreign bank – or are subject to similarly strict prudential regulations in their home country.

Unlike a synthetic ETF, a structured product constitutes a direct derivative contractual agreement between the end-investor (you) and the structured product provider. In other words, rather than the investor necessarily having claim to a specific set of pooled assets that have been set aside, they rely on the contractual obligation between them directly and the structured product provider to provide returns that match changes in a specified index.

That said, there are two types of structured products.

"Collateralised" structured products must provide 100% asset backing, usually in the form of a cash account. That means the daily value of any monies owed to you under a derivatives contract is effectively set aside and held in liquid assets that can be called upon should the counterparty experience financial difficulty.

By contrast, a "synthetic" structured product does not need to provide this cash backing. With this product, investors must rely on the continuing credit-worthiness of the provider to ensure that they get their money back. Accordingly, a collateralised structured product entails greater counterparty risk than a synthetic structured product.

Structured product providers are required to label their products as either collateralised or synthetic. However, adding to potential confusion, structured products can also be described as either exchange traded commodities (ETCs) or notes (ETNs). These *sound* like ETFs but, as should now be apparent, their structure is decidedly different.

It goes without saying that investors should be mindful of the specific type of product structure used by a commodity ETP that they are considering purchasing.

HEDGED VS. NON-HEDGED COMMODITY ETFS

Most commodities in global markets are US dollar-denominated. This means that the $A value of an unhedged currency ETP will reflect two factors: movements in the $US price of the commodity in question, and the exchange rate between the US and Australian dollars.

Should the $A rise strongly at a time when global commodity prices are also rising strongly in $US terms (as generally tends to be the case), currency hedged commodity ETFs will generally perform better than unhedged commodity ETFs.

As noted above, like its gold physically backed ETF (QAU), BetaShares synthetic ETFs are $A currency hedged – allowing investors to make a purer bet on commodity price movements, without worrying that exchange rate trends might move in the opposite direction.

Given that interest rates in Australia are currently higher than in the United States, investors in currency hedged ETFs also currently enjoy the benefit of a yield "pick up." The currency hedge effectively involves borrowing US dollars (at low interest rates) to buy $A (which earn a higher interest rate).

Of course, should US interest rates rise above those in Australia, a currency hedge would then detract from ETP performance. What's more, when the $A is falling currency hedged commodity ETPs would produce lower returns than those that are unhedged.

FUTURES VS SPOT PRICES

As noted above, in many cases, it's simply not possible or practical for an investor to buy a product that directly tracks a commodity's spot price. Instead, commodity ETPs need to rely on futures contracts. Typically, an ETF provider will buy a near-dated future contract (say three months until expiry) to gain exposure to the commodity price in question, and then sell this contract just before it is about to expire and buy another near-dated contract. This process is known as "rolling."

Depending on the relationship between that future's price and the current spot price, however, it means the price performance of the ETP may not always track the "spot" price performance of the commodity in question.

For example, if the futures price is consistently above the spot price (known in the market as "contango"), there will be some capital loss from holding the future contract and selling just near expiration, a "negative roll yield." This will result in the ETP's price performance underperforming the commodity's spot price. Of course, the ETPs price may well still rise over time if the spot price increases more quickly than that which has already been priced into the futures contracts being bought and rolled by the ETP provider.

What's more, when the futures price is *below* that of the spot price (known as "backwardation"), the ETP's price performance will tend to outperform the spot price, due to a positive roll yield.

Perhaps a simple way of thinking about this is that if the market is already expecting a strong rally in a certain commodity's spot price in coming months (say, oil or wheat), it will be harder for a commodity ETP that uses futures contracts to perform at least as well as the spot price.

This issue aside, it should be noted the BetaShares hedged crude oil ETF (OOO) has done a reasonable job of tracking the $US spot oil prices recently. Investors should be aware, however, that this correlation may not hold in some future periods when large expected price changes are already reflected in oil price contract futures.

Performance of WTI "Spot" Oil vs BetaShares Crude Oil Index ETF (OOO)

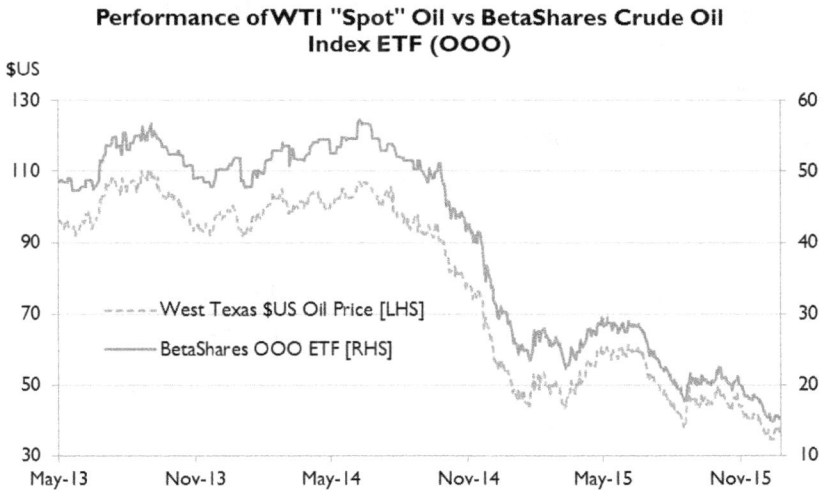

Source: Bloomberg

Overall, commodity ETPs expand the investment choices for local investors. Although at face value they seem relatively easy to understand, it pays to "look beneath the hood" into how they are structured, so as to fully understand likely risks and returns.

FOREIGN CURRENCY ETFS

There are currently five foreign currency ETFs that are available on the Australian market, covering the US dollar, the British pound, the Euro, and the Chinese renminbi.

Foreign Currency ETPs as at Dec 2015						
ASX Code	Product Type	Fund Name	ICR (%p.a.)*	FUM ($m)	# trades	Bid-Offer % spread
EEU	ETF	BetaShares Euro ETF	0.45	$3.9	22	0.15%
POU	ETF	BetaShares British Pound ETF	0.45	$9.1	21	0.12%
USD	ETF	BetaShares U.S Dollar ETF	0.45	$499.0	1,665	0.11%
ZCNH	ETF	ANZ ETFS Physical Renmimbi ETF	0.30	$1.0	3	0.21%
ZUSD	ETF	ANZ ETFS Physcial US Dollar ETF	0.30	$2.6	24	0.21%

As a result, investors also have the option to trade currencies through ETFs rather than by using often more highly leveraged and complex contracts for differences (CFDs), or currency futures.

This can have costs and benefits. The benefit is that investors are less likely to take on excessive exposure and risk, since no leverage is involved. The downside is that sophisticated traders and investors who are able to manage their risk exposures well may find currency trading through ETFs less rewarding (even boring!).

The first three currency ETFs tradable on the ASX were offered by BetaShares. The assets of each ETF are simply held as international bank deposits (with JP Morgan Chase) in the relevant currency denomination. Each ETF charges a management fee of 0.45% for the service. To the extent that these bank deposits earn interest (which given current interest rate levels would not be much), it is not distributed to investors as income, but rather accrues as a benefit to the ETF's market value.

Currency ETFs are probably of the most interest for longer-term investors who either want to have some offshore currency exposure for pure diversification purposes – or who have a strong view that the Australian dollar is overvalued and that foreign currencies are likely to rise in value.

Indeed, likely reflecting expectations that the $A is set to fall further against the $US, flows into BetaShares $US ETF have been most popular to date, with $499 FUM as of the end of 2015.

Of course, investors who believe the Australian dollar is headed for a fall also have the option of investing in unhedged international equity ETFs or commodities, which provide exposure to both foreign markets and global currencies. The S&P 500 ETF (IVV), for example, is valued in $A terms and so provides exposure to both the US S&P 500 equity index, plus the US dollar. If you invest in the IVV and the US dollar rises against the $A, then the $A value of your investment will rise even if the US S&P 500 equity index (in local $US terms) remains unchanged. If you are positive on both global equity markets and negative on the $A, then gaining exposure via the unhedged international equity ETFs may be the way to go.

Otherwise, if you are negative on global equity markets (fearing a global economic downturn) and you believe this will also hurt the $A (perhaps by lowering commodity prices), then you might want to remain more highly invested in cash that is invested in offshore currencies. This is where the advantage of currency-based ETFs is most apparent, by providing a means of diversifying the currency denomination in one's defensive cash holdings.

Moreover, one advantage of seeking foreign currency exposure through an ETF, rather than, say, through a traditional foreign currency-denominated account at a local bank, is significantly lower transaction costs. The buy-sell spreads on a typical foreign currency bank account, for example, have been around 10%, compared with only a 0.2% spread on, say, the BetaShares U.S. Dollar ETF. Even allowing for the ETF's management fee (0.45% p.a.) and somewhat higher brokerage costs, the cost of buying and then selling $10,000 worth of US dollars would be approximately $80 using a currency ETP, compared with $1000 in costs through a traditional foreign currency bank account.

STEP 4:

Developing ETF Investment Strategies

There are various ways that ETFs can be used as part of the investment strategies for both long-term and shorter-term traders.

DIVERSIFICATION WITHIN A SINGLE ASSET CLASS

If you are looking to invest over the longer-term, the simplest ETF investment strategy is to use a broad-based asset class ETF to achieve the "beta" returns usually available from that asset class.

For example, as an investor, you may have decided to only invest in equities. You also know that you should not place all your eggs in one basket. As seen in the chart below, by increasing the number of stocks held, investors are usually able to reduce the volatility of their overall investment returns (toward the market average), without necessarily giving up a lot of expected returns.

That's because the return from individual stocks are not perfectly correlated, so while one is going up another is usually going down – even though both may tend to rise at the same rate, on average, over time. As the saying go, the benefit of diversification is one of the few "free lunches" available in investment markets.

The Benefit of Diversification by Investing in More Stocks

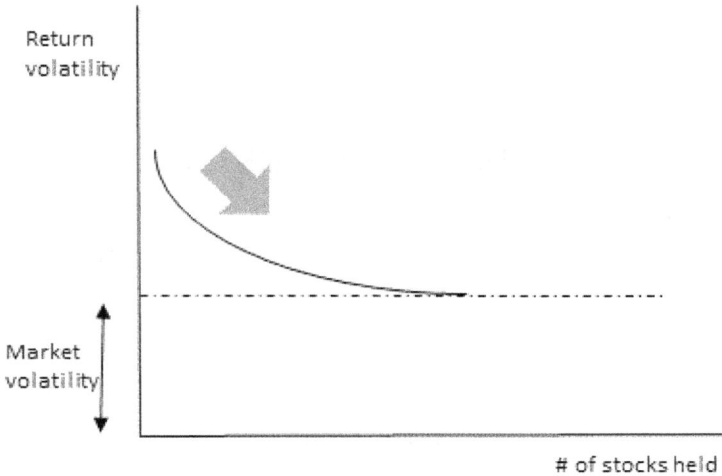

So, let's say for diversification purposes that you have decided to own at least a handful of large cap stocks and a smattering of small cap stocks. You might own a portfolio of perhaps a dozen stocks.

With an ETF, however, you can achieve even broader asset class diversification with less paperwork hassle. This reduces your risk, as well as the administrative time. For example, even if you held a portfolio of five large cap stocks, such as Telstra, the Commonwealth Bank, BHP-Billiton, Westfield, and David Jones, 20% of your portfolio would still be exposed to the ups and downs of an individual stock.

While none of these companies is likely to go broke overnight (though it's still a remote possibility), the volatility in their share prices would still likely be greater than that for the market as a whole. There's always the risk that even one or more blue chip stock could fall on hard times and nose-dive in value over time. Unless you keep a careful eye over your portfolio, there's always a risk one stock could drop sharply in value, leaving you the tough decision of knowing when and if to replace it with another.

You will also have to manage paperwork for five stocks, such as, rights issues, AGM notices, and dividend distributions.

If your aim in holding a handful of blue chip stocks is to achieve broad equity market diversification, however, the same end could be achieved by owning an ETF that tracks the performance of the Australian equity market overall. For example, as of the end of 2015, the largest holding of the S&P/ASX 200 Index was that of the Commonwealth Bank, accounting for 10% of the index. Indeed, the top 4 banks accounted for approximately 30% of the index, with Telstra and BHP-Billiton accounting for a further 5% each.

It is important to note that owning an ETF that tracks a broad-based index removes the difficulty of having to decide when to sell poorly performing stocks. It's the nature of market capitalisation indices that stocks that lose significant market value are automatically cut from the index over time. What's more, smaller cap stocks that gain significant market value – making them a large cap stock – are then automatically added to the large cap indices that ETFs typically track. In this regard, and as noted in the ETF benefits section above, market-capitalisation weighted ETFs indexed to measures of company size have the advantage of *survivorship bias*.

Top Ten Stocks in S&P/ASX 200 Index - Dec 2015

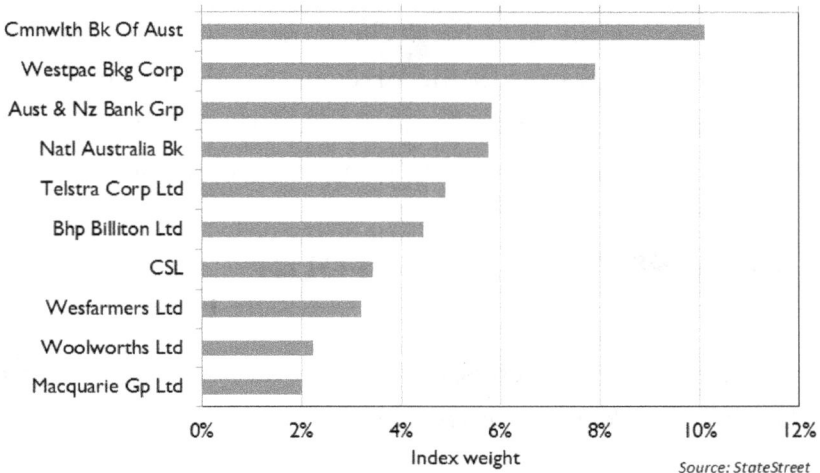

Index weight

Source: StateStreet

As a result, ETFs are a particularly good idea for the portfolios of self-managed super funds (SMSFs) that have tended to prefer direct equity investments due to their lower cost over actively managed equity funds.

What's more, by using a broad equity market ETF to account for a core part of their equity portfolio, investors are then free to focus on more speculative higher risk/higher return stock bets for the rest of their portfolio, since they have fewer stocks to manage overall, and the volatility of their portfolio should be lessened due to better diversification within the core holding.

The same thinking applies to other single asset portfolios, such as ones that consist of corporate or government bonds, or even gold. In these cases, one could likely achieve better diversification and reduced administrative hassle by investing in their asset class of choice partly or completely through an ETF.

Indeed, many retail investors have contemplated gold holdings as part of their investment portfolio. They seem to think (mistakenly) that they need to buy gold bars! These days, an easier and more secure form of exposure to the precious metal can be achieved through simply buying a gold-linked ETF. The ETF provider will effectively hold gold bars on your behalf in a secure vault.

MULTI-ASSET CLASS PORTFOLIO

By investing in one asset class, even on a diversified basis, investors are basically stuck with the risk and return characteristics of that asset class.

As seen in the chart below, for example, equities typically produce the highest long-run returns, but also have the greatest return volatility (as most recently seen during the global financial crisis, when Australian equity returns slumped 38% in 2008). Cash and bonds tend to produce lower returns, but also with less volatility or "risk," as broadly defined. At least over the past decade or so, listed property also had volatile returns, largely due to significant swings before and after the GFC.

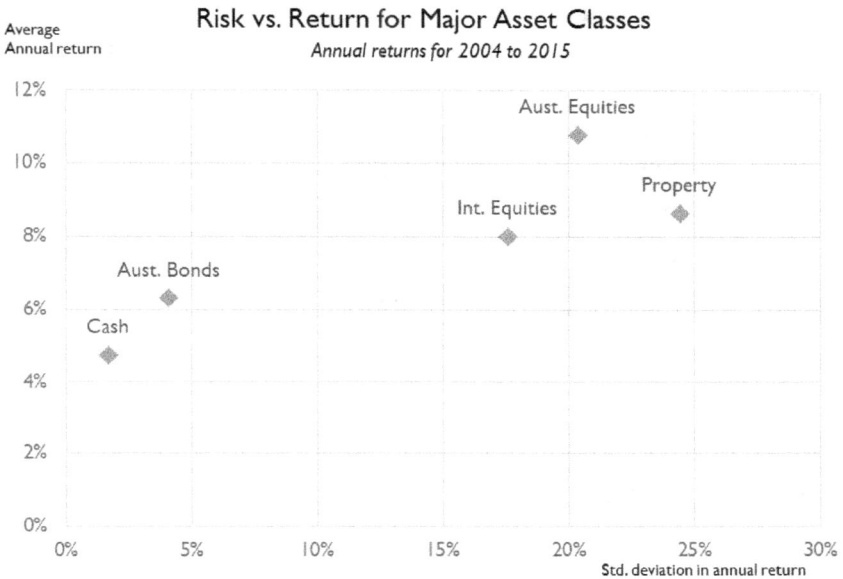

Risk vs. Return for Major Asset Classes
Annual returns for 2004 to 2015

Average Annual return (y-axis): 0% to 12%
Std. deviation in annual return (x-axis): 0% to 30%

Data points: Cash, Aust. Bonds, Int. Equities, Aust. Equities, Property

Wouldn't it be great to be able to develop a portfolio that offers the correct blend of risk and return that you are most comfortable with? By investing across asset classes, that is precisely what *multi-asset class* portfolios aim to do.

What's more, another advantage of a "multi" over "single" asset class portfolio is even greater diversification, allowing investors to reduce risk without necessarily sacrificing a lot in returns.

The key reason is that, as with different securities within an asset class, asset classes themselves trend to perform differently over time. For example, equities tend to do best in periods of strong economic growth with low inflation and interest rates. Bonds do best in high (but falling) interest rate environments, while commodities perform best in high inflation environments.

Indeed, in the 12 years from 2004 to 2015, the correlation in annual returns for Australian bond and equities was negative 0.75. Equities tended to do well when bonds did not, and vice versa.

Blending different assets within a portfolio, therefore, can allow you to better withstand changing market environments. Indeed, research shows that blending different asset classes with low correlation in their returns into a single portfolio can often produce a better long-run return performance – for a given level of year-to-year portfolio return volatility – compared with only owning a single asset class, such as only bonds or equities.

The exact asset blend that is best depends on each investor's relative risk and return preferences.

The table below shows the average annual returns – and the volatility (or standard deviation[16]) in those returns – investors would have experienced had they invested across a range of asset classes over recent years, with weights attached to each asset class varying within their portfolio[17]. The weights used broadly conform to typical weightings used within the financial industry for long-run "model portfolio" for different risk exposure.

---

[16] Standard deviation is a measure of the dispersion in returns around their average rate. If an asset has an average return of 5% and a standard deviation of 10%, for example, it means there's a 68% chance that in any given year, its returns will be within a -5% to +15% range.
[17] This also assumes annual portfolio re-balancing back to asset class weights.

Multi-Asset Portfolios for Differing Risk Levels: *based on returns from 2004 to 2015*					
	Low	Low/Medium	Medium	Medium/High	High
	Asset Weighting per Portfolio				
Cash	15%	10%	5%	5%	5%
Aust. Bonds	60%	55%	45%	30%	5%
Property	10%	10%	10%	10%	10%
Aust. Equities	7.5%	12.5%	20.0%	30.0%	40.0%
Int. Equities	7.5%	12.5%	20.0%	30.0%	40.0%
Defensive	75%	65%	50%	35%	10%
Growth	25%	35%	50%	65%	90%
Annual returns					
Average	**6.8%**	**7.1%**	**7.7%**	**8.6%**	**8.9%**
Std. deviation	3.5%	4.9%	7.6%	11.3%	15.4%

"Higher risk" portfolios with a greater weighting toward equities would have produced the highest average annual returns over this period, but also with the greatest return volatility.

For investors, however, the main point is that there are now several relatively cheap and transparent ETFs that can provide broad exposure to each asset class. Depending on the particular ETFs chosen, average management expenses fees for developing a similar multi-asset class portfolio could be approximately 0.5% p.a., or even less.

For example, relatively young investors with several decades until retirement might opt for a higher risk core portfolio, comprised of mainly equities and relatively fewer lower return cash and bonds. Older investors, either in or close to retirement, however, might prefer a less volatile portfolio which provides steadier annual income returns, as might best be achieved with a portfolio heavily weighted toward cash or bonds.

Further diversification is also possible through including international equities, foreign currencies, and even commodities, such as gold.

ETFs offer a way for investors (especially those running a self-managed superannuated fund) to develop a highly diversified multi-asset portfolio that meets their desired risk-return profile (as decided on either by themselves or in consultation with their financial planners) at an often much cheaper cost than using actively managed funds.

STRATEGIC ASSET ALLOCATION

One issue to consider when developing a multi-asset portfolio is how actively managed you would like it to be over time. Are you a "set and forget" investor, or one who would like to try and *actively tilt* your asset allocation based on market conditions.

Strategic portfolios are those that blend exposures to different asset classes based on the long-run expected risks and returns of each asset class. As such, these portfolios aim to provide the best long-run returns for a "buy and hold" investor, subject to their maximum risk tolerance. Clearly, investors that either can't stomach a lot of return volatility or can't risk a major loss (as they're either in or near retirement) will need to settle for more investments in less volatile (or lower return) assets, such as cash or bonds. Those that can afford to take on more risk can invest in more growth assets, such as equities.

Although expert views differ on the margin, the broad asset allocations referred to in the table above are likely close to what many industry professionals would regard as reasonably optimal strategic asset allocations for different risk levels. As noted above, investors might seek even greater diversification by swapping some Australian equity exposure (usually around one-third to one-half) for international exposure, or allocate 5 to 10% of their portfolio to commodities and/or international currencies.

For long-term strategic investors, all that is then required is to "rebalance" their portfolio at regularly intervals. Opinions differ on the appropriate timing, but a reasonable compromise might be once per year. For example, if equities have done particularly well in a given year (for example, their weight in your portfolio has increased from, say, 50% to 60%), re-balancing would involve selling down some equities at year-end so that their overall weight fell back to 50%. Instead, you would buy exposure to the asset classes that had not done so well, so that their weight in your portfolio was restored to the long-run desired levels.

Annual re-balancing allows investors to take advantage of any short-run *momentum* within asset classes within a given year (which can be a feature of markets), while also eventually reducing exposure to any potentially "overheated" asset classes so that the portfolio remains in line with the investor's risk profile. Annual re-balancing also has the advantage of ensuring any realised capital gains are eligible for a capital gains tax discount.

TACTICAL ASSET ALLOCATION

For strategic investors, the only changes to their multi-asset portfolio over time would be for re-balancing purposes. For tactical investors, however, changes in the asset allocation might also be pursued based on either a fundamental and/or technical analysis of respective asset classes.

For example, your strategic asset allocation might suggest that 60% of your portfolio should be in equities, and 40% in bonds. The tactical *inter-asset class* decision, however, is whether you should invest more or less than 60% in equities over the short-term due to expected short-term asset class returns.

Indeed, although equities might be expected to return 10% per year on average over the long-term, year-to-year asset class returns, however, are rarely smooth. Over any given period (or say 2- to 5-years), it is likely that some asset classes (such as, equities or bonds), will produce returns above their long-run expected average, while other asset classes will produce below-average returns. In theory, if we knew in advance which asset classes would produce the best returns over the short-run, we could tilt our portfolio accordingly and enjoy even higher long-run returns.

Of course, determining which asset classes will perform best over the short-run is not always as easy in practice.

Fundamental or Valuation based strategies

One way to predict likely short-run returns between asset classes is based on valuations.

Most valuation-based tactical asset allocation strategies tend to exploit regression to the mean. When, for example, asset returns have had a strong run, their valuations tend to reach expensive levels. Regression to the mean dynamics then, suggest that a period of below average returns for that asset class is then likely for a few years. Similarly, after a major market downturn which forces valuations to cheap levels, regression to the mean analysis suggests a period of above average returns is then likely.

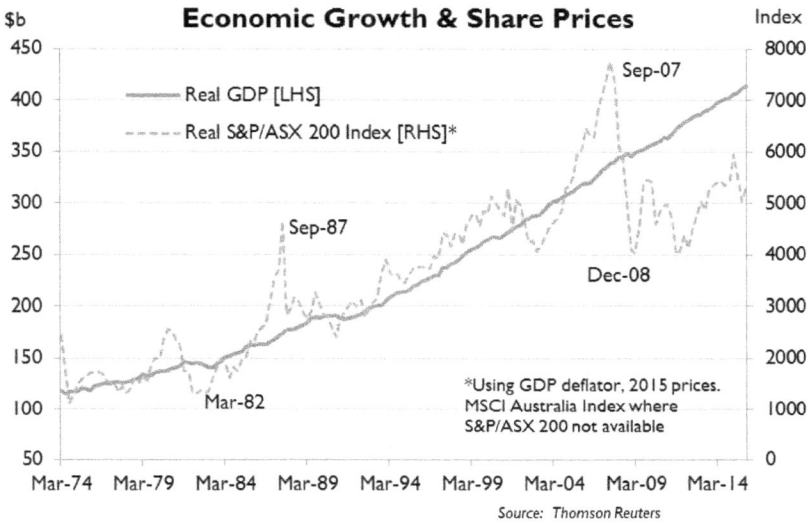

$b	**Economic Growth & Share Prices**	Index

Real GDP [LHS]
Real S&P/ASX 200 Index [RHS]*

Sep-07
Sep-87
Dec-08
Mar-82

*Using GDP deflator, 2015 prices.
MSCI Australia Index where
S&P/ASX 200 not available

Mar-74   Mar-79   Mar-84   Mar-89   Mar-94   Mar-99   Mar-04   Mar-09   Mar-14

Source: Thomson Reuters

As seen in the chart above, Australian equity prices have broadly tracked economic growth over the past few decades – with notable overvaluation in 1987 and 2007, and undervaluation in 2008 and 1982. Equity prices tend to underperform after periods of extreme overvaluation and outperform after period of extreme undervaluation.

As of the end of 2015, it's notable that equity prices have struggled to match recent economic growth, such that on this (albeit crude) valuation measure, equity prices look cheap. Corporate earnings weaknesses, following commodity price declines since 2011, have helped hold back equity prices. All else constant, that would suggest that a period of "catch-up" above-average market returns could be due.

As seen in the chart below, the share-price-to-GDP ratio, as a broad measure of likely future returns, has not been that bad historically.

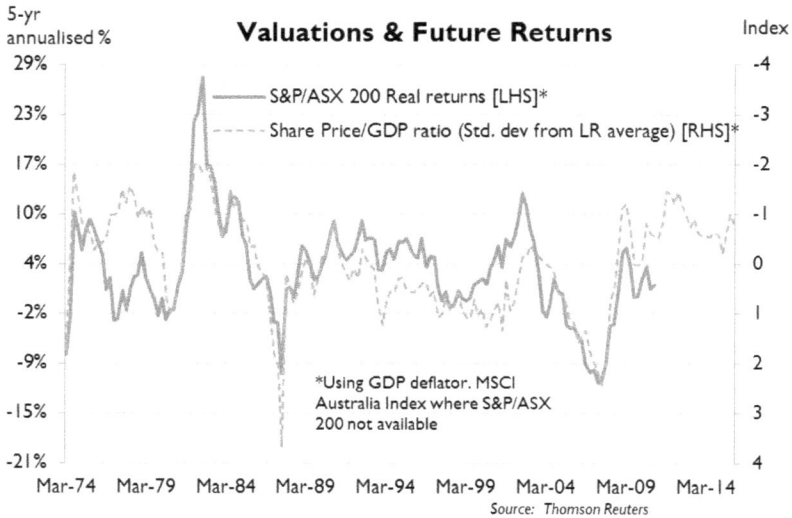

Valuations & Future Returns

— S&P/ASX 200 Real returns [LHS]*
---- Share Price/GDP ratio (Std. dev from LR average) [RHS]*

*Using GDP deflator. MSCI
Australia Index where S&P/ASX
200 not available

Source: Thomson Reuters

That said, share price weakness relative to GDP in recent years has meant this valuation measure has tended to overestimate actual share price returns. In the 5 years up until the end of 2015, for example, annualised real share prices returns were only 1.4%, whereas this valuation indicator would have suggested real price returns in the 4-10% range.

As regards tactical asset allocation, using this valuation measure – or other more preferred precise measures – could suggest that a period of above average equity returns is ahead over, say, the next 5 years. In this case, you might tactically decide to *increase* weight to equities and *reduce* weight to other assets within your portfolio. The benefit of using ETFs is that these tactical asset allocations can be easily achieved with only a few trades.

The same broadly holds true for other asset classes, such as bonds and commodities. Interest rates and commodity prices also rise and fall over time and can reach extremes. This can result in periods of above-average returns, followed by periods of below-average returns for each asset class.

As concerns bond markets, for example, global bond yields are currently very low and are generally expected to return to "more normal" levels over the next few years. In this case, investors will lose out by investing in bonds not only because of low current yields, but also because of likely capital losses on their holdings, as and when interest rates rise. Assuming "regression to the mean" in bond yields also holds, this would suggest an underweight tactical allocation to bonds.

Commodity prices, meanwhile, are still correcting from very high levels reached a few years ago. In real terms, for example, gold prices are still well above their long-run average levels, suggesting further prices weakness ahead.

One qualification with value-based approaches is that regression to the mean may take several years to play out – and the timing is generally uncertain - whereas over shorter periods, there is a risk that momentum or market "irrationality" can keep expensive asset classes rallying, or vice versa. As Keynes once said, "the market can remain irrational for longer than you can remain solvent."

Another cautionary note is that regression to the mean assumes that valuation levels that prevailed in the past *will* prevail in the future. This may not be the case if major structural changes have taken place in an economy (such as lower inflation reducing interest rates to sustainable new levels well below past averages).

All that said, a rough rule of thumb that likely still holds true, is that periods of exceptionally strong asset price returns are likely to be followed by a period of weak returns – and vice-versa – as apparent in the 115 years of Australian equity returns in the chart below.

All Ords Past vs. Future Annualised Returns: 1900-2015

Following 5-&
10- year returns

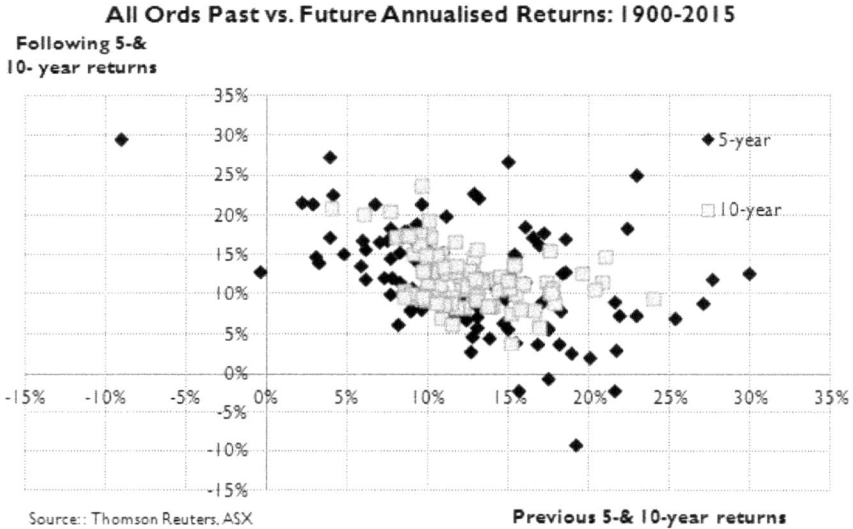

Source:: Thomson Reuters, ASX

Previous 5-& 10-year returns

Momentum & Trend based strategies

Another more mechanical option is to make tactical switches between asset classes relying on relative price momentum and/or trending behaviour.

Indeed, financial research suggests that *momentum effects* – or the tendency of asset classes (or asset class sub-segments) that have performed strongly (poorly) over the *recent* past to keep performing well (poorly) for a while longer - are evident in many markets. This happens because markets can be slow to recognise and adjust to new fundamentals, and also because often "herd-like" behaviour can develop among investors.

In essence, asset prices seem to be driven by momentum in the short-term, but by valuations over the long-term. These two forces are reconciled by corrective "regression to the mean" periods, which push prices back to fair-value once momentum has driven them too far (either to the upside or downside).

In fact, if momentum effects become too strong, it can create "bubbles," where valuations reach extreme levels. This often results in large jarring corrections at some stage. America's dotcom bubble earlier last decade is one such example.

Related to momentum investing is *trend investing*, such as only investing in an asset class that is trending up based on, say, whether current prices are above or below a moving average of past prices. Trend signals could also be used in place of relative performance in choosing between investments, i.e., invest in one investment choice when the *ratio of its price* relative to that of an alternative investment choice is trending up.

Of course, the trick in trend or momentum investing is to jump on an identified wave as early as possible – and also try to get off before it comes crashing down! In choosing a time period, there's a trade-off between being sure that an apparent shift in relative performance is not simply noise, versus having a signal early enough to profitably act on it.

Longer-term time periods (say one or two years) suffer from lags. This means that one can miss out on an early trend and hold on too long once a trend changes. Investing in something that has performed well for numerous years also exposes oneself to the risk of a corrective "regression to the mean" period. Indeed, it is often noted that past investment performance is not necessarily an indicator of future performance. In fact, it may be a potentially better indicator of a *poor* performance ahead!

Very short-term trends, however, (say a few days to a few weeks) may be too erratic – meaning one may overreact and jump on trends, just as they are about to change once again. This problem is known as "whipsawing."

Most research on momentum investing tends to find that a past performance period of between *six months to one year* tends to perform best, in terms of being most likely to predict the relative strength of returns over the next month or so.

A simple momentum and trend-based rotation strategy

As an example, what follows is a simple momentum-based strategy for tilting asset class allocation over time. Let's say you have a strategic asset allocation in place, but want to ear-mark, say, up to 30% of your portfolio for a momentum-based tactical asset allocation overlay.

The chart below outlines the results of combination momentum and trend-filter strategy relative to a benchmark strategy of simply placing equal allocation across seven investment options of cash, bonds, equities, resources, financials, world equities, or gold (the latter two both being currency hedged).

Decisions are made at the end of each month. The "momentum model" allocates 50% of funds to each of the top *two* investments based on the past six-month price performance, provided that prices are *also above* their 10-month moving average. Where either one or both of the top two performing investments have prices *below* their 10-month moving average, spare funds are placed in the equally-weighted portfolio instead.

As shown, the models outperform the equal-weighted "buy and hold" portfolio, particularly over the past ten years. Over the past 10 years up until the end of 2015, the equal weighted buy and hold portfolio produced annualised returns of 3.3%, compared with model returns of 10.0%.

Asset Allocation Trend & Momentum Models

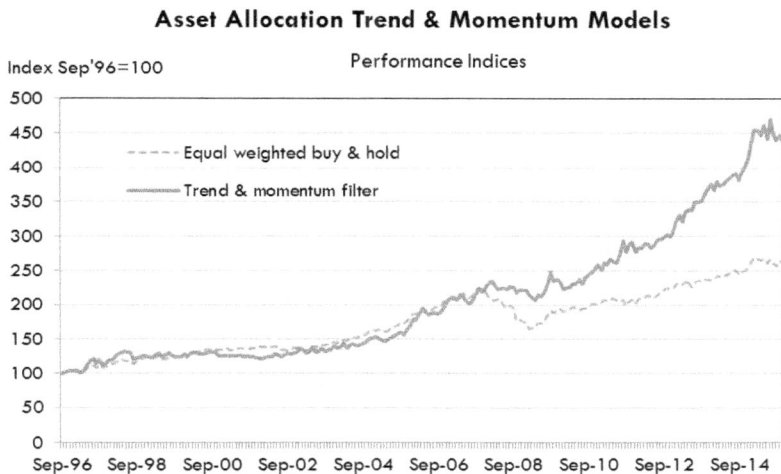

Note: Past performance is not an indicator of future performance.

Drawdown Curves

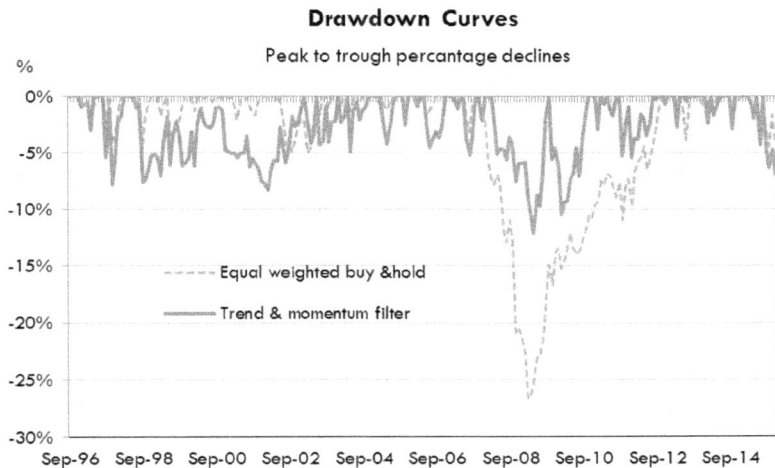

Note: Past performance is not an indicator of future performance.

Equally importantly, the model resulted in *less downside risk* for the portfolio, as evident in the "drawdown curves" shown in the chart below. The worst peak to trough drawn down for the model was 12% in early 2009, whereas the equal weighted portfolio maximum drawdown was 26%.

Note, however, that that trend/momentum models as depicted above can result in high portfolio turnover, and therefore, trading commission costs and more regular capital gains taxes. Assuming a 0.1% trading commission (CommSec's cheapest online rate), then even turning over the portfolio 5 times per year, however, would cost 0.5% of the portfolio's worth.

Some caution on momentum models

The idea of only investing in markets when prices are trending up and/or showing good relative price momentum sounds appealing, but caution is still required when using these strategies in practice.

Why? As with using historic valuation indicators, one problem with timing or momentum rules is that *while they may have worked in the past, they will not necessarily work in the future* if the nature of market dynamics change.

Indeed, trending models work best when markets trend strongly, rising smoothly for several months to several years, before reversing and falling for several months to years. Many market-timing services like to point out that a simple 200-day moving average rule would have caused investors to exit the equity market before the worst of the past two serious bear market downturns, in the early 2000s and 2008.

This is true. However, such a rule could also cause investors to return to the market late, after it has already posted strong gains. These lost gains must be set against the losses avoided during the downturn to know if you gained from the exercise.

What's more, whenever markets fail to trend strongly – and tend to move sideways – market timing rules can result in losses, due to selling when the market drops modestly, only to then miss the market rebound, because you're in cash. These losses are known as *market whipsaws.*

To avoid these problems, market timing rules can be made more complex, including using a range of technical indicators, such as moving averages, overbought/oversold signals, and trend filters. But, the more complex the model, and the more it is tweaked to fit past data, the bigger the risk that the model suffers from *look-back or optimisation bias,* and is unlikely to work as well going forward.

The simpler the model, and the more evidence of its success beyond the period for which is was created, the better.

Another issue is that the more one trades in and out of a market, the less likely one is to receive dividends (which account for around half the returns on the Australian equity market), and the more capital gains taxes and brokerage costs that will need to be paid each year. Investing in cash will at least earn a cash return. Dividends are also still possible if switching from one equity sector to another.

An extensive analysis of timing models gives rise to the following conclusions. For starters, most timing rules (especially an equity vs. cash decision alone) are *unlikely* to outperform a simple buy and hold strategy over the very long-term, due to the problem of lost dividends, whipsaws during trendless periods, and late entry once markets rebound from bear periods.

Assessing these models against the Australian equity market may not be the fairest comparison, as these models may also reduce downside risk. Perhaps the best comparison is the risk/return trade-offs offered by timing/momentum models compared with other portfolio allocations (such as a blend of cash and bonds) that offer similar downside risk protection.

Timing models may well be able to outperform even the equity market, however, once options, such as leverage and/or shorting, are considered. For example, instead of just buying equities when the trend is up, one might borrow and invest more in the market, such as via the BetaShare's GEAR Fund. Similarly, instead of just going into cash when the equity market trend turns down, one might also short the equity market, say, by buying the BetaShares BEAR fund.

The downside, however, is that while long-run returns from such a strategy can be enhanced, the *volatility* of returns – and the periods over which the timing model underperforms – are larger.

Of course, another option is to buy a managed risk ETF (see the section above), which use systematic rules to reduce the volatility of equity investment returns and cushion downside risk.

It's *best to see timing models as either a complement or substitute for other risk/return portfolio strategies*, such as holding a component of your portfolio in bonds or cash. The issue is really what risk-adjusted returns an investor is most comfortable with, and what strategy – either conservative asset allocation and/or market timing – can best achieve it.

CORE/SATELLITE INVESTMENT PORTFOLIOS

Some investors may decide that they want to try and add an "alpha strategy" overlay that attempts to beat the benchmark performance of one or all core indexed asset class investments in your portfolio. In this case, ETFs also then lend themselves to another complementary strategy, core/satellite investing.

The idea behind core/satellite investing is to first use low cost index funds (such as ETFs) to achieve, at a minimum, the "beta" returns from each asset you seek to be exposed to. This is the "core" portfolio element. The second, or "satellite," element of the portfolio is to add some portfolio "tilts" within one or more asset classes to try and generate extra "alpha" returns within each asset class.

Core/Satellite investing has several benefits. Most obviously the approach allows for more granulated risk control. What you're doing is effectively unbundling the "beta" (or market) and "alpha" (market beating) returns from a certain desired asset class. By investing in an index fund, you know exactly how much of your portfolio will be "beta" and track a certain asset class – and so how much exposure you may then wish to allocate to "alpha" investments that may be more volatile, but offer potentially higher longer-run returns within that asset class.

With active funds, you never can be too sure of your beta vs. alpha portfolio exposure, especially if the fund's senior managers and/or investment strategies change.

By retaining core beta exposure, moreover, you can also probably afford – at the margin – to consider more aggressive (though volatile) active investment opportunities that may have an even lower correlation with your beta investment holdings, and be more likely to outperform over time.

Passive vs. Active Managed Funds

One source of alpha investment exposure you could seek is via an actively managed fund – assuming that you can find one you are happy with and are confident might offer market-beating returns.

For example, if you decide you want 60 per cent of your portfolio to be in Australian equities, the traditional approach would be to allocate, say, 20 per cent to three separate actively managed funds. Each fund would be expected to at least provide returns that matched the market, plus a little extra "alpha" return. You'd then watch each one carefully and swap funds when and if you thought that one fund was not doing its job, or you had a specific new investment theme (such as resources or global markets) that you wanted to pursue.

A core/satellite approach, however, might instead invest, say, 45 per cent of the money earmarked for equities into a single low cost "core" equity ETF, and the remaining 15 per cent equity allocation among the preferred actively managed funds, which are known in this case as equity "satellites." As seen in the charts below, the overall equity allocation remains 60% in each case, though there's clearer separation between alpha and beta components with the core/satellite strategy.

This approach has numerous advantages. For starters, it can help reduce management fees. By buying an actively managed fund, you might be paying a high management fee to a manager, even though a good chunk of their return is only beta.

Traditional Equity Allocation

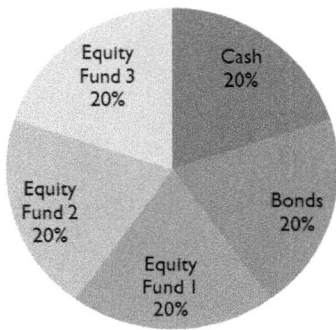

- Cash 20%
- Bonds 20%
- Equity Fund 1 20%
- Equity Fund 2 20%
- Equity Fund 3 20%

Core/Satellite Equity Allocation

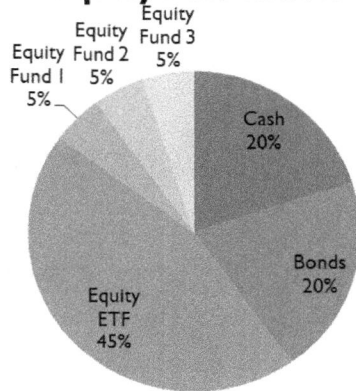

- Equity Fund 1 5%
- Equity Fund 2 5%
- Equity Fund 3 5%
- Cash 20%
- Bonds 20%
- Equity ETF 45%

You might instead get this beta return with a lower cost ETF. For example, if all three active funds charged a 1.5% management fee, and an equity ETF charged only 0.25%, then allocating three quarters to the ETF and one quarter among the active funds would reduce overall equity management fees to 0.56% – more than halving the cost.

Another advantage is that core/satellite investing also saves on transaction costs and taxation, if you decide to swap active managers. For example, if your portfolio contained 20 per cent of an active fund that consistently lagged the market, then selling it for something else would involve turning over one-fifth of your portfolio. But, if due to a larger index fund holding, the active fund only accounted for 5 per cent of the portfolio, then making the change only involves turning over a much smaller portfolio share with lower transaction costs and lower potential capital gains tax to pay.

Of course, while you might leave decisions over how to beat asset class benchmark returns to an active manager(s), you might also try to do it yourself, through various *intra-asset class tilts*. In this case, ETFs can provide both the core *and* satellite parts of your portfolio.

EQUITY MARKET TILTS

So far, we have discussed using ETFs to gain diversified exposure to a single asset class, or multiple asset classes. We have also looked at strategies for switching *between* different asset classes over time.

We now turn our attention to *intra-asset* class investment strategies, i.e., strategies that might allow your equity or bond market investments to outperform the overall equity and bond market.

Most obviously, one classic strategy involves picking stocks that might outperform the market. But, as we'll see, many investment themes implicit in an investor's choice of stocks can also be represented through specific equity-related ETFs, thereby avoiding any stock specific risks associated with thematic investing.

TRADE MARKET VIEWS WITH A MARKET ETF

Indeed, one problem with stock picking is that the day-to-day movement in stock prices is often heavily influenced by overall market movements. Even if you could pick great stocks, the market often does not reward investors for their effort, as stocks are sold down whenever the market gets into trouble.

If you are buying stocks because of an overall view of the market, a market ETF will more easily do the same job.

Using market ETFs to invest instead is a bit like applying the 80/20 rule. As seen in the chart below, investment research regularly finds that most movement in individual shares (especially large caps) over a few days to a few months is largely driven by the overall market, and to a lesser extent by individual corporate performance. As a result, investors might reasonably decide to just trade the market, and avoid the extra research effort required for individual companies, given the often relatively low extra marginal return that this provides.

Share Price vs. S&P/ASX 200 Index
Quarterly % changes betweeen Q1-2007 and Q4-2015

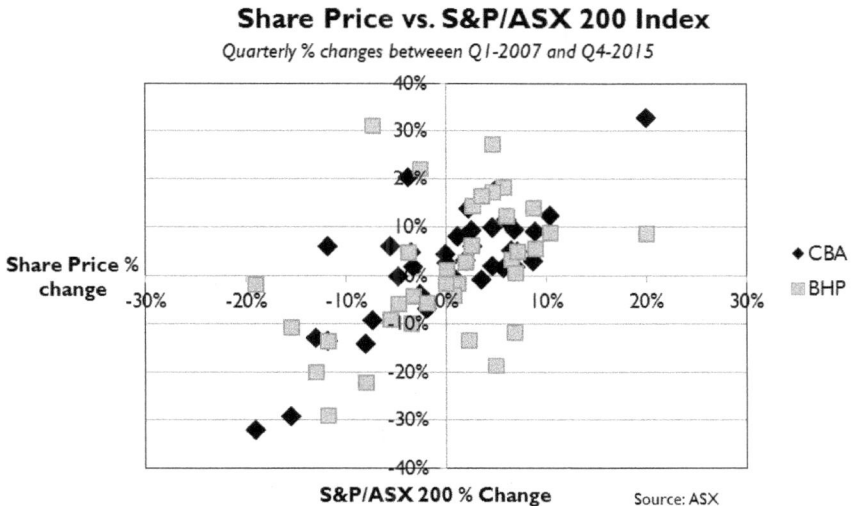

S&P/ASX 200 % Change   Source: ASX

From a technical and fundamental perspective, moreover, trading ETFs may be easier, since there will be less price performance "noise" over time. For long-term investors, future earnings growth for the broad equity market and industry sectors should be more stable and predictable compared with that of individual companies. After all, we know that the broader economy grows approximately 6 per cent in nominal terms on average each year – which is a reasonable estimate of long-run earnings for companies across the whole market.

It is important to also note that by diversifying exposure across numerous companies, investors are less exposed to the illiquidity of individual stocks – and the risk of being unnecessarily "stopped out" of positions by excessive price movements, which can be caused by false rumours or predatory trading by large professional traders.

If a stock has a well-known technical price support level, for example, it is easier for a large professional trader to sell down the stock in the hope of triggering (sometimes automatic) stop-loss sales by nervous smaller retail investors. The large trader makes money on the gap down in the price, and then buys back shares to close out their position. Investors may be stopped out of their trade only to watch the share price then bounce back up again. Due to the need to move many stocks at once, such manipulation is less easy to achieve with broad-based ETFs.

It should be noted that the majority of ETFs that track most international equity markets, such as the S&P 500 in the US, are still "unhedged" and valued in $A terms. This means that investors take on currency exposure when investing in these offshore markets. If the $A rises, it will reduce offshore market returns.

Short-term trading, of course, is not for everyone. It requires a lot of time and skill, and at the end of the day, many active investors may find their returns are not worth the trouble.

Apart from trading the overall market, there are also a range of other equity market themes that could be played through ETFs.

THEMATIC EQUITY TILTS

Financials vs. Resources

For example, you might decide that you want more exposure to a certain industry sector.   The S&P/ASX300 Equity Index has a relatively heavy weighting of 40% to financials (excluding listed property), and just under 15% (largely resource stocks) to the metals & mining sector.   It has less than 1% exposure to information technology stocks, and only a 5% weight on consumer discretionary stocks.

As noted above, there are now numerous domestic sector ETFs on the market, though they (at this stage at least) largely cover only the market's financial and resources sectors.   That said, the dominance of financials and resources on the Australian market still lends itself to a few potential sector investment strategies.

For starters, as seen in the chart below, financials have tended to outperform the market when interest rates are falling. Lower interest rates encourage more credit demand and sales activity for major banks.

By contrast, financials tend to underperform when interest rates are rising, due to the slowing effect on credit growth and the economy, and concerns over rising bad debts. Financials have tended to outperform, for example, since the latest interest rate cut cycle began in late 2011.

Financial Sector & Interest Rates

%

Ratio: S&P/ASX 200 Financials ex A-REITs to S&P/ASX 200 [LHS]

180 day bank bill yield [RHS] - inverse axis

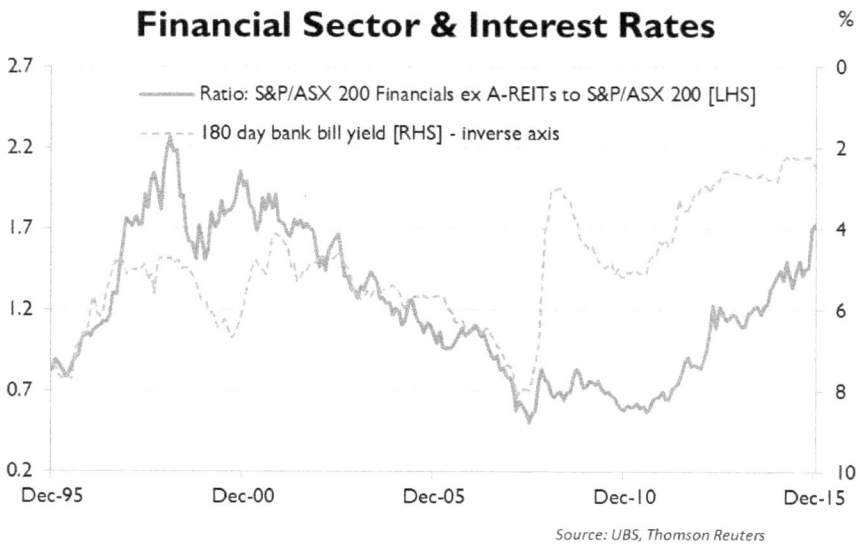

Source: UBS, Thomson Reuters

By contrast, as seen in the chart below, the resources sector tends to outperform when commodity prices are rising, since this boosts mining company profits. The resource sector enjoyed a long period of outperformance during the commodity price boom earlier last decade, but has tended to underperform since the commodity price peak in mid-2011.

Since they account for such a large share of the Australian market, *simply getting the sector call on "financials versus resources" correct may go a long way in helping you outperform the market.* In turn, these sector calls largely depend on the likely direction in both interest rates and commodity prices. If you have a strong view on either, this could then be expressed in a sector preference, using a sector-based ETF.

Index Resources Sector & Commodity Prices

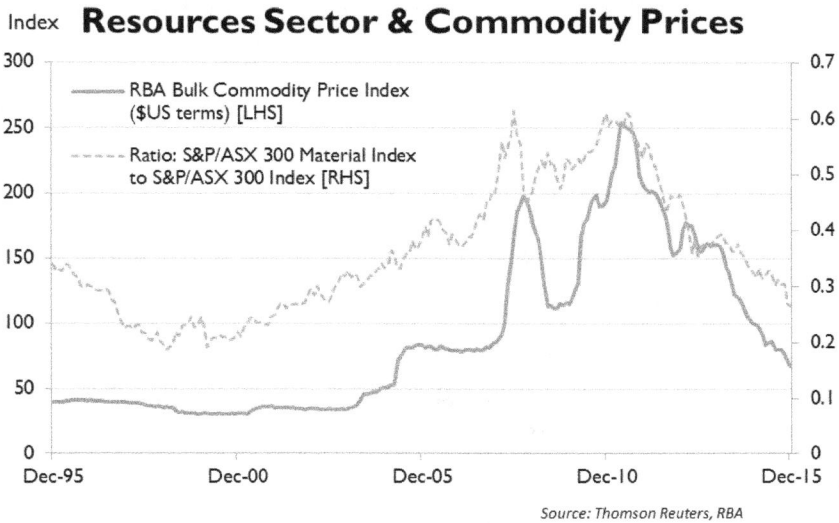

Source: Thomson Reuters, RBA

More generally, the key point is that it's rare for all sectors to move together in any given bull market. Certain sector themes tend to dominate, either over the whole cycle or at least during certain stages.

High Dividend Stocks

Other sector tilts currently available in the Australian market are listed property, high dividend yield stocks, value, and growth stocks. Over recent years, for example, a major Australian market theme has been the outperformance of high dividend yield stocks due to low interest rates.

If you believe that this theme may continue, you have the choice of either trying to find high dividend yielding stocks on your own or – for a relatively small management fee – buy one or more of the several high dividend yield ETPs now listed on the ASX, or even simply a financial sector ETF.

Even if these ETPs only track the broader market in price terms, outperformance should still be possible, at least to the degree that they maintain an above market average dividend yield.

Small vs. Large Caps

Another tactical option is the switch between large cap and small caps, depending on your view of relative trends. As seen in the chart below, and perhaps surprisingly, small caps have not consistently outperformed large caps on the Australian market – at least since the mid-1990s. This likely reflects the strong performance of our concentrated banking sector and major mining stocks over time. Over the past two decades, Australia has enjoyed first a credit boom (favouring financials), followed by a mining boom (favouring resource stocks).

Small Caps Relative Total Return Performance

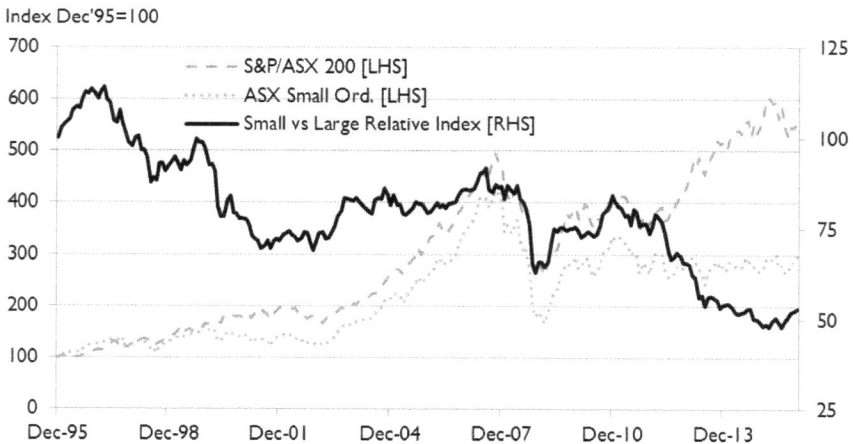

Index Dec'95=100

- – – S&P/ASX 200 [LHS]
- ········ ASX Small Ord. [LHS]
- —— Small vs Large Relative Index [RHS]

Source: UBS, Thomson Reuters

That said, small caps do enjoy periods of outperformance, usually during early stages of a cyclical bull market. This happened in 2003 and 2009. The downside is that small caps tend to fall harder during downturns. Small caps notably underperformed during the recent market upturn since mid-2012, reflecting investor hunger for safe high-yield blue chips, such as the banks and Telstra. That said, they then enjoyed a period of outperformance in the second half of 2015, as both major mining and bank stocks faced difficulties.

Domestic vs. International Equities

Another potential investment tilt could be between domestic vs. international markets. As seen in the chart below, global markets outperformed Australia in the late 1990s when the dotcom boom was underway and Australia was under-represented in technology stocks.

World vs. Australian Equity Performance

Index Dec'95 = 100   MSCI All Country Index vs S&P/ASX 200

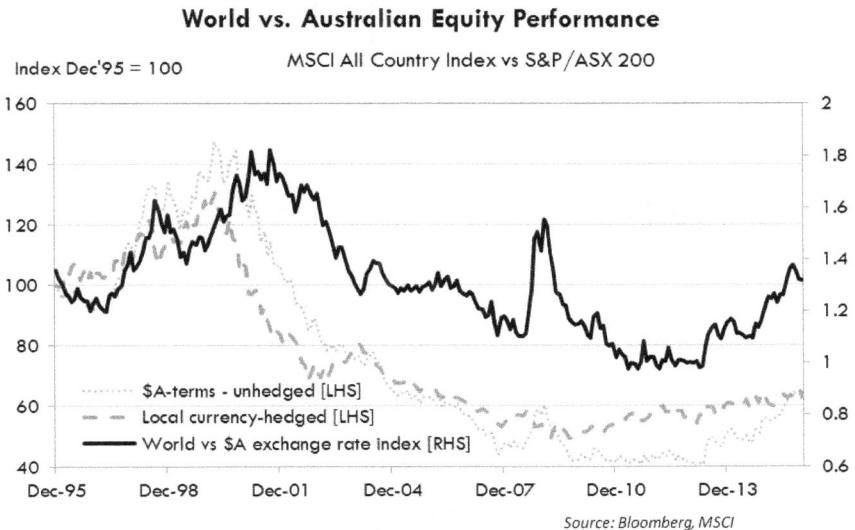

Source: Bloomberg, MSCI

Australia outperformed when the dotcom bubble burst. This outperformance continued as the rise of China and the commodity price boom got underway in the early 2000s. Australia also initially outperformed coming out of the GFC, but relative performance has turned negative in recent years since the commodity price decline.

Indeed, international equity outperformance has been even stronger in recent years in unhedged terms, due to the decline in the $A.

International tilts might also be used when certain global investment themes don't favour Australia, such as strong equity performance in emerging markets and/or strong growth in the information technology sector (which has an extremely small weight on the Australian market). Indeed, if you did not have a strong view on likely currency trends, but believed global equities were cheap relative to those in Australia – and so set to outperform – you could tilt your portfolio toward an international (hedged) ETF.

As evident from the previous section, there is a broad range of international equity ETFs available on the ASX. If you were bullish on equities, but also had the view that the Australian dollar was set to fall, you could tilt your portfolio more toward international (unhedged) equity ETFs to benefit from the rise in their currency value against the $A.

Relative performance gyrations over recent decades highlight the value of portfolio diversification and how ETFs make it much easier to tilt one's portfolio, according to currency and sector trends.

Should the $A continue to trend lower and/or other industry sectors – such as IT again – begin to take off globally, it's likely that global markets will continue to outperform Australia, both in currency hedged and unhedged terms.

It is important to note that ETFs also offer the option for investors to tilt their portfolio to particular offshore regions – such as Europe, Asia, or emerging markets – or particular countries, such as Japan, the United States, China, South Korea, Taiwan, or Singapore. Indeed, in recent years investors would have done even better internationally with a specific focus on the US market, which has outperformed Europe, Japan, and even emerging markets.

Emerging markets

As seen in the chart below, in hedged currency terms, emerging market equities broadly outperformed Australia during the China/commodity boom in the decade prior to the financial crisis.

EM vs. Australian Equity Performance

Index Dec'95 = 100   MSCI All Country Index vs S&P/ASX 200

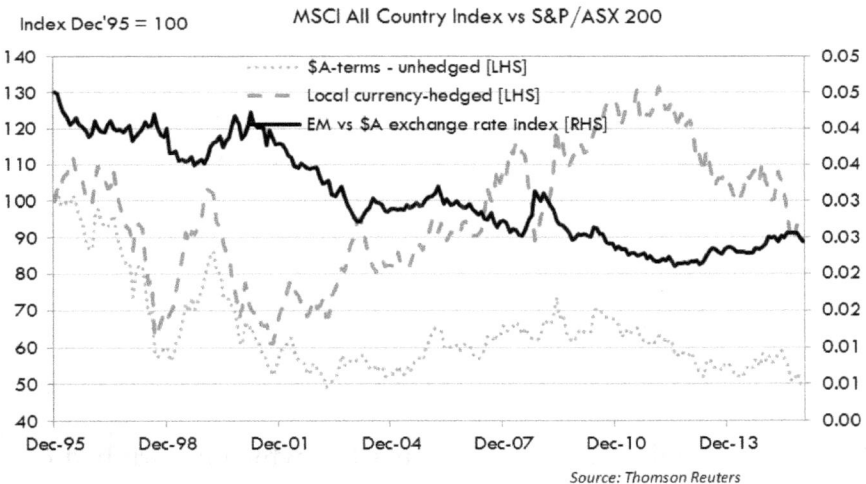

Source: Thomson Reuters

This outperformance generally continuing after the volatility associated with the financial crisis had passed. Since 2012, however, emerging markets have underperformed due to China's slowdown and the commodity price decline. More recently, a rising US dollar and the fear of higher US interest rates have added to concerns surrounding emerging markets, due to the risk of capital outflows. These relative performance trends have been more muted in unhedged currency terms, as emerging market currencies tend to track the $US, which has weakened during the commodity price boom, but has strengthened more recently.

China

China is an interesting country-specific play. As of the end of 2015, the Chinese equity market remained in the throes of a correction, after bubble-like price surges over the previous year.

Performance of China ETF (IZZ)

$A price

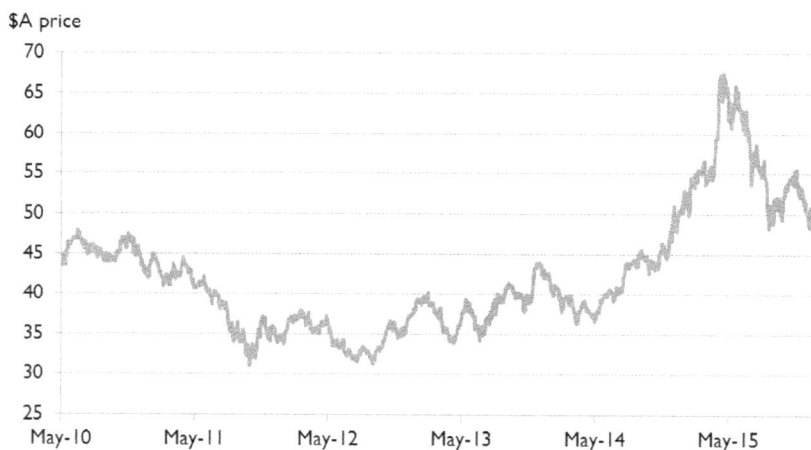

Source: iShares, Thomson Reuters

This, in turn, followed a long bear market, which in turn had been preceded by another bubble-like surge in prices prior to the global financial crisis. Suffice it to say that the Chinese share market is highly volatile!

The Chinese currency – the renminbi – is still closely pegged to the US dollar, and so is likely to rise in value against the Australian dollar, if the Australian dollar continues to fall against the US dollar.

With global commodity prices past their peak, and global commodity supply rising, it would not be surprising if the equity markets of net-commodity *consuming* countries, like China, fared better in coming years than those of net-commodity *producing* countries, like Australia.

Global Sectors

There are also several global industry-sector ETFs available. From ishares, three currently cover relatively defensive sectors, such as telecommunications, health care, and consumer staples – and all are unhedged.

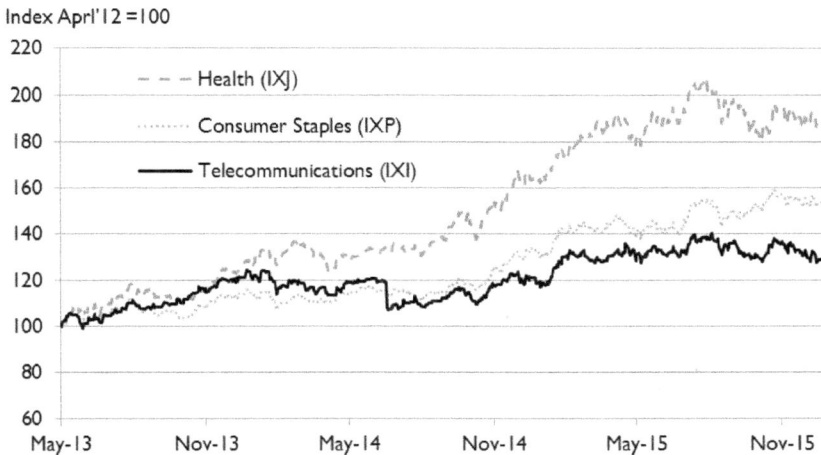

Global Sector ETFs*

Index Apr'12 =100

Source: IShares, Thomson Reuters

Of these sectors, global health care at least might be an interesting option to get diversified exposure to a sector likely to benefit from population ageing globally.   Indeed, the health care ETF has outperformed the local Australian market very well over recent years, though relative performance has consolidated somewhat since mid-2015.   As noted earlier, over July and August 2016, BetaShares also launched currency-hedged global sector ETFs covering the banking, gold mining, healthcare and internet security sectors.   Once again, they are also locally domiciled.

NASDAQ-100 Index

Although not strictly a "sector" ETF, another option to consider in this light is the NASDAQ-100 ETF (NDQ), given the relatively high weight it places on the technology sector.

NASDAQ-100 vs. World MSCI ex-Aust*

Relative Price Indices

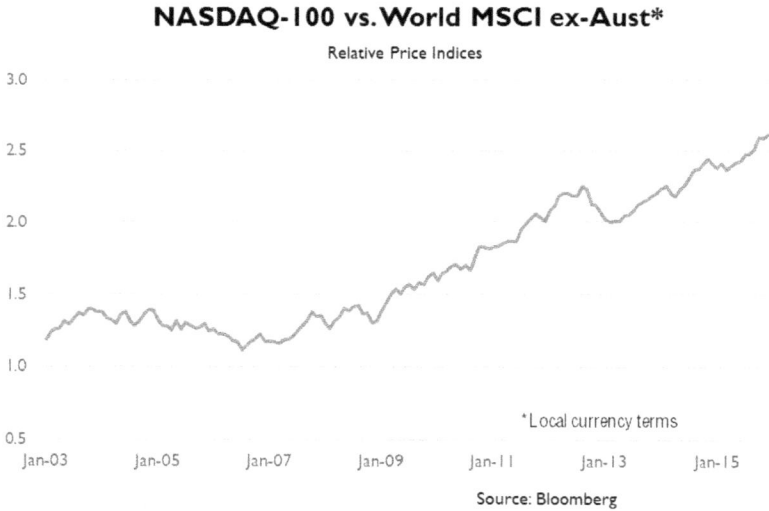

*Local currency terms

Source: Bloomberg

The NASDAQ-100 Index has had a particularly impressive run in recent years – even outperforming global markets – thanks to strong growth in earnings by tech heavyweights, such as Apple, Google, Amazon, and FaceBook. Indeed, as a result of this strong earnings growth, unlike during the late 1990s dotcom bubble, price-to-earnings valuations for the NASDAQ-100 Index even by the end of 2015 were still close to long-run average levels.

The NASDAQ-100 Index, however, is not just about technology. As of the end of 2015, technology accounted for 55% of the index, while consumer discretionary and health care sectors accounted for an additional 20% and 15%, respectively. Technology only accounts for around 1% of the Australian market, and health care and consumer discretionary only account for a further 5% each. In this sense, the NASDAQ-100 provides particularly good international sector diversification – and in some high growth areas – against the Australian market.

BOND MARKET TILTS

Given the range of bond market ETFs available on the market, investors also have the option of tilting their fixed-income exposure in certain directions – such as favouring corporate bonds over government bonds (credit bets), or inflation indexed bonds over non-indexed bonds (inflation bets).

Corporate vs. Government Bonds

Several ETF providers offer a choice between bond ETFs that include just government bonds or "composite" indices that also include corporate bonds. Russell also offers a pure corporate bond ETF, RCB.

As seen in the chart below, in times of heightened financial market stress, corporate bonds tend to be sold off more heavily than sovereign government bonds (due to the latter's higher risk of default), which can result in the yield on ETFs containing corporate bonds (such as those that track the Bloomberg Composite Index) rising relative to those that contain government bonds alone.

UBS Composite vs Treasury Index Performance

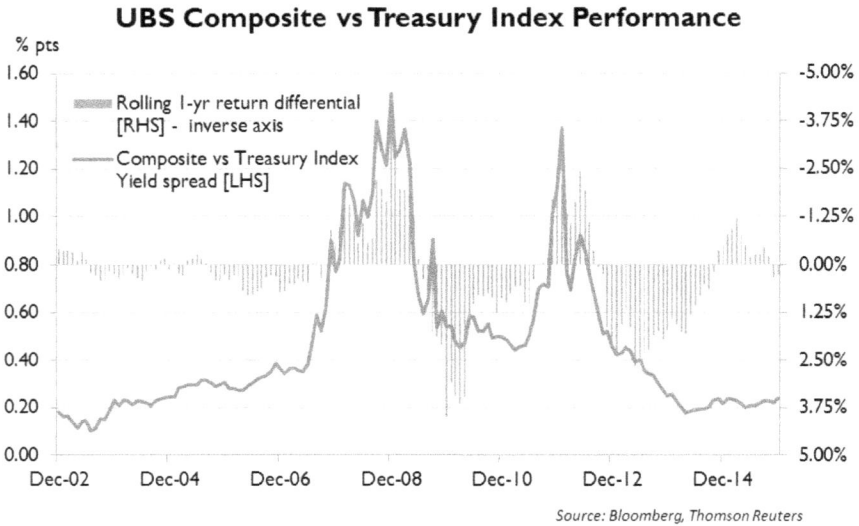

% pts

Rolling 1-yr return differential [RHS] - inverse axis

Composite vs Treasury Index Yield spread [LHS]

LHS	RHS
1.60	-5.00%
1.40	-3.75%
1.20	-2.50%
1.00	-1.25%
0.80	0.00%
0.60	1.25%
0.40	2.50%
0.20	3.75%
0.00	5.00%

Dec-02   Dec-04   Dec-06   Dec-08   Dec-10   Dec-12   Dec-14

Source: Bloomberg, Thomson Reuters

In turn, this surge in yields causes the corporate bond and broader composite bond ETFs to underperform government bond ETFs. But, this underperformance unwinds when financial panic subsides. Over the past few years, credit spreads have contracted as investors have chased yield, causing the broader composite bond index to outperform the narrower Treasury (Federal Government) bond index. The modest widening in corporate spreads in the past year has led the composite index to marginally underperform the Treasury bond index.

These credit cycles provide tactical switching opportunities for a nimble investor.

If you think that credit risk premiums are too low and set to blow out, you might consider increasing exposure to relatively safer government bond ETFs, over the composite or corporate bond ETFs.

However, once you feel the investment panic has become over-done, it might be an opportune time to increase bond market weighting to ETFs with higher corporate bond exposure – to lock in both high yields and gains from extra capital appreciation, as yields eventually fall back towards more normal levels.

What's normal? Recent history suggests the fair-value yield gap between the UBS Composite and Treasury bond index is around 0.8%. If the gap spikes above 1%, it favours tilting back toward the composite index.

As of the end of 2015, the yield spread between the UBS Composite Bond index and the Treasury index was relatively low, suggesting that investors are not being greatly rewarded for taking on the added risk of corporate bond exposure. There is a risk, therefore, of corporate bond underperformance should global financial market panic start up again.

Nominal vs. Inflation Protected Bonds

As noted earlier, investors have a choice between bond ETFs that are either indexed or not indexed for inflation. The former have their principal value indexed over time to the inflation rate. As a result, the current yield differential between bonds not indexed to inflation (nominal) and those that are indexed to inflation is a measure of the market's longer-run inflation expectation, less a (usually small) "liquidity premium" attached to nominal bonds (due to their greater market depth and tighter trading spreads).

As seen in the chart below, the yield differential between nominal and inflation-indexed bonds can vary widely over time. However, it has tended to average approximately 2.5%, or in line with the RBA's 2 to 3 per cent inflation target. In this sense, the market views the RBA as competent at its job, and its inflation target is a credible projection of what inflation is likely to average over the next 10-years.

Inflation Indexed vs Nominal Bond Returns

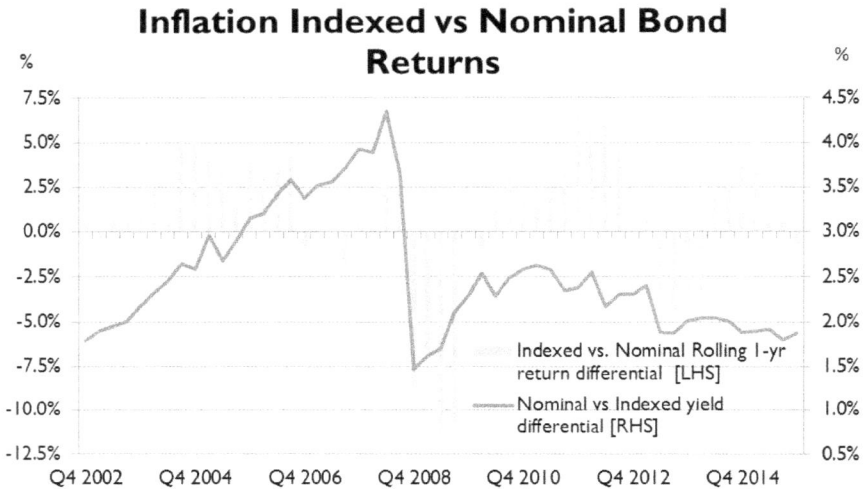

Source: Bloomberg, Thomson Reuters

However, inflation indexed bonds have tended to produce *better* returns than non-indexed bonds over the past decade or so, apart from when nominal bond yields declined sharply during the GFC. Post GFC, indexed bonds outperformed non-indexed ones, as the yield differential returned to more normal levels.

As of the end of 2015, the market's yield differential between nominal and indexed bonds remained 2% - or relatively low by historic standards. As a long-term investor, if you fear that inflation is likely to be significantly higher than 2%, (it is important to note the RBA is targeting 2.5%), it would pay to allocate some funds to indexed bond ETFs to hedge against risk. By contrast, if you think inflation will remain very low – or there's even a risk of deflation – you would be better off avoiding indexed bond ETFs in preference for the high yields offered on nominal bond ETFs.

More short-term traders, meanwhile, can look to exploit tactical switching opportunities as they arise - due to changes in the indexed/non-indexed yield differential over time. Assuming that long-run inflation holds at approximately 2.5%, the above chart suggests that it is opportune to switch to inflation-indexed bond ETFs when the yield differential between nominal and indexed bonds is relatively low (such as 2% or less) and switch to non-indexed bond ETFs when the yield differential is relatively high (greater than 3.5%).

Local vs. International

As noted above, returns from the Australian and global fixed-income benchmarks have tended to be closely correlated in recent years, as global long-term bond yields across countries also tended to move together (broadly).

That said, to the extent that the trend towards a decline in interest rates and inflation since the late 1980s has largely levelled out, there is probably greater scope for differences in local and international fixed income performance in the coming years. Generally speaking, when interest rates are likely to fall more aggressively in Australia relative to overseas, Australian fixed income ETFs are likely to outperform international fixed income ETFs (and vice versa).

There is also scope for tactical allocation to high-yield international fixed income ETFs when global credit risk spreads have ratcheted up to relatively high levels – as happens following market panics or recessions.

AD-HOC STRATEGIES

CASH EQUITISATION

Cash equitisation is a strategy for investors who have new large funding sources to place in the market, but are not yet quite sure which specific investments (i.e., individual companies, ETFs, or managed funds) they want to make. Until these decisions are made, placing funds in a broad index tracking ETF can avoid potential *cash drag* should the market rise before specific investments are made.

TAX LOSS HARVESTING

ETFs may provide a means for investors to realise the loss on a specific investment for tax purposes – such as offsetting a capital gains tax liability - before year end, without losing exposure to the overall market or the sector in question.

For example, an investor sitting on a loss on Commonwealth Bank (CBA) shares may wish to recognise this loss with a sale before June 30. But, should investors quickly re-buy CBA shares, the tax loss claim could be denied by the Australian Tax Office (ATO) on the basis that the sale was solely for tax purposes and there was no significant change in asset exposure.

Under this strategy, it might be possible to instead buy an Australian equity ETF – or even a financial sector ETF – in place of CBA shares, at least in the interim. That way, investors retain some exposure to the market or a specific sector without potentially incurring the wrath of the ATO – especially if the argument is made that the switch was for non-tax purposes, such as greater portfolio diversification.

Of course, using this strategy also requires careful tax advice and/or consultation with a licensed financial planner.

CONCLUSION

Although the first ETF was launched in Australia more than 10 years ago, the market is still in its infancy by the standards of other developed markets (such as in Europe and the United States).

With the growth in self-managed super funds and moves by the financial planning industry to abolish product commissions, however, we are probably on the cusp of a major upsurge in ETF investor interest and product offerings.

As we explained in this book, ETFs – when used correctly and carefully – can greatly help investors in simplifying and lowering the cost of their investment strategies.   With Australia's ageing population and strains on the public pension system, it is vitally important that more Australians maximise their retirement strategies.

That said, the relative infancy of the Australian ETF industry also means it is still enjoying an "age of innocence," where the product offerings are still fairly simple, and, in the main, still merely try to cover the major asset classes that should form the core of most investment portfolios.

Over time, however, the range of products on offer should grow, adding to not only to choice, but also to the complexity and potential cost that face investors. In their competitive quest to offer more enticing products, ETF providers are likely to slice and dice investment markets ever more finely. A greater range of actively managed ETPs are also likely on the horizon, where product providers aim to beat investment benchmarks using specific investment strategies (such as, value and/or momentum).

As complexity grows, it will be important for investors not to lose sight of the original benefits of ETFs – namely, their low cost, transparency, and diversification opportunities.

That being said, with this knowledge now consolidated into this handy book, I hope many investors and financial planners will now feel more comfortable and excited about fully incorporating the myriad benefits of ETFs into their investment strategy.

Viva the ETF Revolution!

www.ingramcontent.com/pod-product-compliance
Lightning Source LLC
Chambersburg PA
CBHW060552220326
41598CB00024B/3079